The librarians' book on teaching through games and play.

Andrew Walsh

D1375237

The librarians' book on teaching through games and play.
Andrew Walsh

ISBN (paperback): 978-1-911500-07-0

Published by Innovative Libraries, 2018.
Sepapaja tn 6
Lasnamäe linnaosa,
Tallinn, Harju maakond
15551
Estonia

UK contact address:
195 Wakefield Road, Lepton, Huddersfield. HD8 0BL
andywalsh@innovativelibraries.org.uk
http://innovativelibraries.org.uk/

Acknowledgements

Thank you to the Higher Education Academy (now Advance HE) for commissioning me to write a report for them on my experiences of game based learning and giving me permission at the contract stage to re-work it into a book. Some of the material in this short book is based on that report, which can be found at http://eprints.hud.ac.uk/id/eprint/26570/

Dedication

To George's Shaun the Sheep who is always up to mischief and keeping us on our toes.

Introduction

Over many years now I've attempted to bring an increased component of game based learning into the teaching of information literacy skills. I've also brought elements of 'playfulness' into my teaching practice that will be outlined here too. There are serious pedagogical reasons for this, and I go a little into the theory later in this book, but I'll focus on how my own practice has developed, give some examples of games you could adapt and re-use, and I'll give some tips for bringing similar techniques into your own learning and teaching practice.

But why should you care? Why should anyone else consider developing their academic practice in a similar direction? For me, I see games and play as great for three different areas: as a flavour of active learning, as a chance for learners to explore ideas in a safe and playful environment, and as a way of increasing engagement with the subject matter. Games often aren't all three of these, but can be any one or more of them!

Games can be online, but I more often use physical, printed games. They can be quick and easy learning activities dropped into an overall session, rather than the sole focus of a lesson. They are familiar to most people, young and old, regardless of background, all of which makes them easy to "slip" fairly painlessly into your overall teaching repertoire.

What about me? Why should you pay any attention to what I say? I work part time at a UK university with the job title of 'Teaching Fellow" within the library. I'm also a UK National Teaching Fellow, Fellow of the Higher Education Academy, Fellow of the RSA, writer, trainer, game maker, and all sorts of other things… most importantly however is the job my daughter described me as doing to her friends. I'm "a librarian who teaches grown-ups how to play". I now count that as my most important job, being a Playbrarian.

The first part of this book gives some theory and explanation of play and games, which will help you to use this approach effectively and perhaps to argue for its adoption in your workplace. The second part is practical examples of activities that can be adapted and used directly, though you'll find it easier to make these work if you read the first part too!

I hope you enjoy this book and that it encourages and enables you to bring more play into your work.

Play and games

The separate strands of games and play, playfulness, and gamification may be distinct in pedagogical approach, but are also complementary and part of an overall mix of teaching approaches used within my practice.

I teach staff, researchers, taught postgraduate and undergraduate students from a range of disciplines, but the expected learning outcomes are often quite similar. As a librarian by profession, these tend to be focussed around developing the information literacy[1] skills of the target group.

Sometimes the skills we are aiming to develop in the sessions I deliver are fairly low level and primarily routine or factual information skills. We may want students to become more aware of the services that the library offers, or how to access some of those services in person or online. Often, however, the skills we are trying to develop in those sessions are more generic and higher level in nature. Instead of trying to teach students how to access a database, they may be learning how to construct a meaningful search strategy that will work regardless of platform. The students may be learning how to *evaluate* information they have found, or *critically read* that

[1] Information literacy is the ability to think critically and make balanced judgements about any information we find and use. It empowers us as citizens to reach and express informed views and to engage fully with society.' (CILIP, 2018).

material, rather than simply finding a set *number* of resources. A first year undergraduate may learn the basics mechanics of using our main search tool, but later on will need higher level skills such as analysing the journal articles they find and extracting key arguments from them.

Low level skills help to get the students that I see started as library and information users, but they also need a range of higher level skills to become independent learners. The mid and high level skills, however, are of limited use until they are put into the subject and academic context in which they are expected to operate. Often even the lower level information literacy skills and the 'factual' things I get called upon to teach will also only be fully useful with that meaningful context too. Without a meaningful context provided by past experience and the subject area being studied, the students simply do not transfer the skills (or factual matter) into their academic or professional practice. They stay compartmentalised as "library skills" which may be seen as pointless and irrelevant, so are never thought of again.

I use games and playfulness as a route towards enabling the students to apply the skills and facts gained during my sessions to their own academic and professional contexts. I find these approaches a valuable way to bring that context in from their wider practice to the learning of these information literacy skills and ensure that they become part of their academic or professional practice, rather than staying as irrelevant "library skills". In addition, I use these approaches to provide a wider range of sensory stimulation to aid memory formation, to aid in differentiation in teaching and learning in my classes, and occasionally just to inject a little fun into my teaching practice.

I've gone through some more of the benefits of using play, particularly with Higher Education, in a book chapter that was created in the form of a comic. The book is a little hard to get hold of, but my chapter is freely available! (Walsh & Clementson, 2017)[2]. It is also included as an appendix to this book.

---

[2] OA version of the chapter can be found at: http://eprints.hud.ac.uk/id/eprint/31686/

How this practice evolved

These practices developed out of my early experiences of teaching information literacy skills as a new subject librarian. With limited teaching experience and no teaching qualification, I found I was expected to teach these skills to undergraduates, postgraduates, researchers and staff. The materials shared with me, and the classes I observed, suggested that the 'normal' way of doing so was largely didactic in approach, with slides that were talked to, some demonstration of 'how to search databases' and perhaps an element of time for students to 'practice' where they were expected to enact the steps demonstrated in order to carry out searches on their own.

I found this unsatisfactory on both personal and professional levels, with both myself and the students being bored and seeming to learn little. What little learning did take place seemed to be largely on a surface level, with students copying what I had shown them and little real change taking place in their information literacy practices.

Thanks to some colleagues, particularly at professional conferences, I quickly picked up on the idea of taking an active learning approach. Instead of learners passively listening (or not listening) to me talking at them from the front of a classroom, this approach meant that they had to be actively engaged in their own learning. I built a toolkit of active learning approaches and used them widely in my own information literacy skills sessions, bringing benefits to the students and making the teaching experience more satisfying for myself. Together with Padma Inala, I pulled a number of these together in a previous book (2010). Incidentally, my experiences of having this book commissioned and published through a traditional publisher was a big influence on me to publish in more accessible and affordable ways in future.

Several of these techniques that I used fairly early on had game like elements to them, including quizzes and the induction by crossword described in this book. Many of the games I use stay within the spirit of these activities and are short enough to be dropped into any session I deliver as one component of an overall class.

While still thinking about active learning approaches, rather than games, I carried out a project, Lemontree[3], within my library service to gamify the use of the library and its resources, which was designed and delivered by an external company[4]. While this was quite lightweight gamification, offering badges, points, and leaderboards as elements to engage students with the library, the project gave me the confidence to look again at my active learning techniques through the lens of play and games. I've written more about Lemontree and the benefits that such gamification projects can bring to a library elsewhere, particularly related to how they can increase engagement and influence desired behaviours (Walsh, 2014).

---

[3] https://library.hud.ac.uk/lemontree/
[4] www.rith.co.uk

Reflecting my teaching practice in the light of this experience, I allowed it to become more 'playful' and to allow some of the elements I used to teaching particular information skills to become 'games' in their own right.

Even though I wanted to do this, I was still unsure whether information literacy games would be one step too far for my institution, and service, and I was sure they wouldn't be willing to pay for the design and printing of such a game. I therefore side stepped official approval and funding, instead aiming to raise a small amount of money through crowdfunding to create a game, SEEK!, through Indiegogo[5]. This raised enough money to pay for a brilliant librarian with graphic design skills (Tanya Williamson) to take my specifications, flesh out the questions, and create a finished and printable game. It paid for the design work, the printing (initially through a print on demand game company, Game Crafter[6]), and the distribution of games as rewards to the crowdfunding backers.

The game was prototyped and playtested using colleagues in my workplace, before being committed to print with the final designs, questions, and wildcards that we tweaked through prototyping in order to get the balance of the game correct. It was then made available under a Creative Commons licence

---

[5] https://www.indiegogo.com/campaigns/seek-a-game-for-information-literacy-instruction

[6] https://www.thegamecrafter.com/

through Jorum and my institutional repository[7] as print on demand versions, together with editable question cards so that anyone can create their own version of the game. I've since tweaked the question cards and design to overcome issues we found since the initial playtesting.

The same basic process, without the crowdfunding element, has been repeated whenever I wanted to create new learning games. I've become more confident in identifying suitable learning objectives, then designing a game that meets those objectives, prototyping and playtesting the game several times, involving graphic designers where possible to create a workable, good looking design to print and then sending the game to be printed. Students, including placement students and interns in my workplace, as well as recent graduates have been a great source of affordable graphic design expertise and I have used them wherever possible to create more polished games than would otherwise be possible. Even though this can be cheaper than more established graphic designers, it should *always* be paid for, rather than expecting skilled people to do the work for "exposure".

For initial batches of card based games, I have often used flexible business card printers (such as moo.com) rather than professional game printers, to create small volumes of cards for limited expense. If and when I ever want to make a game available for others to buy, I'd then switch to professional card printers, a few of which have the flexibility to print small runs

---

[7] http://eprints.hud.ac.uk/19345/

of card decks. Printing cards and other materials properly, particularly from "proper" card printers make the games look and feel much more professional and help to increase engagement with the materials.

As I've continued to create games, so I have become more confident in bringing in less structured play, such as the collage activity and model making activities described here. These have similar (often wider) benefits, though not identical, and take a similar pedagogic approach, but can require more confidence to use as they are less structured and controlled than more formal games.

I've also used a particular type of game, which I outline later, called escape rooms. These are normally rooms in which a team of people are locked, requiring them to work together to solve a series of puzzles to finally "escape" the room within a time limit. The first time I took part in an escape room I found myself locked in a badly lit room for an hour, with no idea what was going on or how I could use any of the information around me. I couldn't help thinking that this was similar to how students must feel in a typical first year induction! So I started experimenting with them soon after.

Escape rooms tend to have a strong narrative and happen in a strictly controlled area. They encourage people to step into the "magic circle" of play quickly and effectively, so seem to be a good way of encouraging play within a session. I normally use the idea of a box or a table containing everything is part of the game world, making it easy to step inside the game, as well as fairly portable to carry to where I want the students to play it. It might not be quite as effective as a dedicated room, but seems to have a similar impact, mainly as it is so clearly demarcated from the rest of the "normal" world.

I run through an example of an escape room activity and how educational escape rooms might be created later in the book.

To spread the use of games in information literacy instruction, I now run workshops regularly, where attendees learn how to take a similar approach within their own teaching practice. These are most often based around general non-digital learning games, but I also run slightly different workshops focussed on creating educational escape rooms. Workshops last half a day, or full day, with a high degree of group work, resulting in each group producing their own learning game through the same methodology I use. Prototypes created at these workshops are then shared through a blog[8], in the form of short videos.

Please feel free to take any ideas from the blog and re-use them, that is why we share them after the workshops!

_____

[8] http://gamesforlibraries.blogspot.co.uk/

The theory

Game Based Learning is situated in different educational and pedagogic areas. I sketch out some of these below, which may be useful in situating the reader's own practices and providing a framework for developing them. Ideas of active learning and constructivism (particularly social constructivism) appear throughout the practices and are central to the whole approach. In addition to this, theories of games and play are important to the construction of the activities and have benefits in addition to the active learning approach taken. If you know some of the theory behind using games, you can take full advantage of them as a learning methodology. Last, but not least, the idea of embodied cognition, that we think with our bodies as well as our minds, is important in many of these activities, particularly the more creative ones, and will be described in the context of Lego Serious play that inspired the model making activities.

Active learning

My favourite description of Active Learning has always been 'learning by doing' (Gibbs, 1988), perhaps because I tend towards simple definitions anyway, but primarily because it is a great summing up of the core idea of active learning. Students engaged in active learning, who are actively doing, discussing, questioning, playing, describing, creating rather than sitting back passively, are able to work things out for themselves and develop better, more in depth understanding, than if simply presented the same information. This is the core of constructivism, the construction of models of knowledge by the learner themselves, and so active learning is clearly a constructivist approach to learning (Pritchard, 2008). Active learning builds on the learner's existing relevant knowledge and skills, and uses these to make sense of new challenges that the educator presents. It therefore focusses on the process of enabling, or scaffolding, that development of knowledge rather than the learning outcome on its own. Active learning does not feed information to students, but explicitly makes sure students take an active part in their own learning processes (Chickering and Gamson, 1987; Pritchard, 2007).

Active learning, in using existing knowledge and building upon that foundation, is more fluid than more didactic styles of teaching, encouraging discussion and participation between groups of learners, as well as learners and the instructor. Other similar approaches such as problem based, enquiry led, and student centred learning may be seen as more focussed versions of active learning (Chalmers, 2008) but from the same pedagogic stable. This active learning approach sits underneath a lot of approaches I take in the examples within this paper, but through the lens of playfulness and games, which takes the active learning approach in a particular direction.

Play tends to be a social activity and naturally trends towards social engagement and negotiated positions, even in competitive games, so playful learning often tends towards suiting social constructivist ideas of learning, where understanding emerges from the group, rather than just in any one individual. This particularly suits developing the information literacy of students, as this is highly contextual in nature, depending on the subject area and activities of the learners. Play can help information literacy to develop as the group begins to understand what the information *skills* they may be learning mean in the context of their practice. They become information literate in a way that suits their course, profession, or subject area, not in a way that we may wish to impose as librarians.

Games and Play

Building on the active learning approach, games and play have particular benefits in the types of learning I am trying to encourage. The literature on adult learning and play tends to be slightly fragmented depending on the type of games or play being described, but here I will outline some ideas of what play and games are, what they may be particularly good for, and why that has influenced my adoption of them within my teaching practice.

Definitions of games and play can be problematic, partly as everyone has an opinion on what a game actually 'is', so long complex definitions may actually be less helpful than a sketchier, more practical one. This is explained well by Caillois & Barash (2001), where Caillois brings play and games together on a spectrum of play forms. Instead of an activity being pure play, or a formal game, all game and play like activities sit somewhere on this overall spectrum.

Image: An example spectrum of play forms, with apologies to Caillois. Not to scale.

An incredibly formal and structured game, such as chess, may sit towards one end of it, the 'Ludus' end in Caillois' terms. Completely free imaginative play that a child may do with her friends is the opposite end of the spectrum, the 'paidia' end. So playful activities and formal learning games sit on different spots within the same spectrum, and share similar characteristics. What varies are the characteristics that may be dominant within that particular activity. That said, I will give some definitions of play and games that may be useful and show where they sit within my teaching practice.

I find the definition of play by Brown (Brown & Vaughan, 2010, p. 17) particularly useful as it defines play using a list of key features. It states that play is:

> Apparently Purposeless (done for its own sake);
> Voluntary; has Inherent Attraction; Freedom from time;
> Diminished consciousness of self; Improvisational
> potential; and Continuation desire.

The particularly powerful ideas for learning in my examples, are those attributes of a 'diminished consciousness of self', and 'improvisational potential'. These allow the leaner to express ideas and to create new knowledge (such as within the journal collage and Lego activities) in a safe environment. They have the freedom within that activity to approach it in their own way and improvise in how they pull the information together and the playful nature of the whole activity means they are less aware of themselves and braver in expressing their own ideas. These attributes are the key ways in which games, and particularly the playful end of the games / play spectrum, create a 'magic circle' which provide safe places to learn and explore, often through the use of metaphors (Francis, 2009; Gauntlett, 2011).

I take advantage of the safety that play (and games) enables, as I often only see students for 'one-off' sessions, perhaps two or three times through their whole time at university. I introduce new ideas that I want those students to reflect upon and work out themselves how those ideas fit within their current practices as groups of students, or in their future professional practice. This fits in with the explicit argument that play is particularly important at transitional periods as social learning groups, in new situations and in learning new ideas. It provides *"a non-threatening forum for experimentation and a means to form a cohesive subculture/group in which the student feels a sense of belonging or relatedness"*. (Cooper, 1996, p. 33)
Even within the more formal games I use, such as SEEK!, I often find that students will adapt the rules themselves as they play to suit the group dynamics at the time. The safety that

play enables within the game allows them to feel safe doing so, allowing them to explore the ideas contained within the game in different ways.

Games can be thought of as play with more formal rules (rather than improvised rules), but instead of giving a full definition here, I instead give one that can help when thinking about creating learning games. Jane McGonigal (2012) says that *'All games share four defining traits: a goal, rules, a feedback system, and voluntary participation.'*, so when creating a game bear in mind that there should be a clear goal in mind, game mechanics that move us towards that goal (the rules), and a feedback system (so you can tell if you are moving towards the goal).

At this point, I should emphasise that games can have concrete benefits in their own right, such as the opportunity to practice skills, even when reluctantly taken part in by people unwilling to play. The fullest benefits, however, come to those that have entered that state of play, described as entering the magic circle elsewhere as a convenient short-cut. As such, I now tend to see games as being most useful as a vehicle for enabling play, and encourage playful behaviour through those games. This means not sticking to the rules, or firm mechanics mentioned above, but allowing the playful behaviours to emerge that may mean that the players change the rules so that they work better for them.

As the late, great, play master Bernie De Koven said:

In a Game Community, the rules and officials decide if the players are good enough to play. If not, they change players. In a Play Community, the players decide if the game is fun enough to play. If not, they change rules.[9]

For me, we want to be encouraging the play community in our lessons, not a game community (in Bernie's words), which cannot be changed to suit our learners.

Lego Serious Play

The use of model building, such as the Lego activity, is just a specialised case of play. It has the same benefits of play in the provision of a safe environment, a 'magic circle' in which participants can step outside of themselves to explore difficult ideas and concepts. Lego Serious Play (for more details see: Kristiansen & Rasmussen, 2014) came from a research group associated with the Lego company. The inspiration behind it came from two areas that they combined, play and embodied cognition. They wanted to reap the benefits of play, as outlined above, in encouraging the creative exploration of business strategy, including within the Lego group itself.

One of the researchers read a book by an American neurosurgeon, Frank Wilson (1999), which introduced to the group the idea that we think with our bodies as well as our minds. People problem solve by picking objects up and manipulating them, so a learning process that includes an

---

[9] *www.deepfun.com*

element of thinking through our hands (or bodies) can give better results than pure 'intellectual' problem solving.

The two ideas, play plus 'thinking with our hands' (or embodied cognition, see Wilson, 2002 for further explanation), together form the core of the Lego Serious Play methodology[10]. Lego Serious Play creates a safe environment for participants to build metaphors representing ideas or problems. As it was created through the Lego company, it should be no surprise that the medium they choose to build those models was Lego bricks. That said, they work well for such activities, providing a massive range of building options with pieces that most people find easy to put together. Within Lego Serious Play, there are set processes to facilitate problem solving, as well as specially created Lego sets, so although the model making I carry out is inspired by this methodology and overlaps considerably, it is definitely not official Lego Serious Play.

It is hard to explain the process effectively, and it really needs to be experienced and explained as you undergo the process yourself. For an idea of how it works, however, Blair and Rillo (2016) have produced a fairly clear book of examples. Please don't try to use it as an instructor yourself until you've experienced it though, even with the help of the Blair and Rillo book! Without skilled facilitation it may do more harm than good, as it can be a difficult process to run without experience.

The model making and collage activities I have described

---

[10] http://seriousplaypro.com/docs/LSP_Open_Source_Brochure.pdf

above come from the same pedagogic backgrounds as Lego Serious Play. They sit on the more 'playful' end of the spectrum between free play and formal games. They take advantage of the 'magic circle, enabling safety and creativity in participants, while also bringing in similar elements of embodied cognition, in respect of meaning problem solving partly through using our hands. The building of models, or moving pieces around a table that have been cut from a journal article, allow participants to work out their thoughts partly through physical manipulation.

Whether I focus on 'playful' activities, or the more structured games, depends upon the focus of my learning objectives at the time. The structure and sometimes repetition of facts and ideas within games such as SEEK! or induction by crossword, can suit objectives where I may want to introduce facts; allow practice through repetition; or introduce ideas for later discussion. The more formal and structured a game is, the less it allows exploration of ideas.

The opposite is true for the most playful activities. The freer the play, the more the activity allows exploration of concepts and reflection upon prior knowledge, but the less it allows the introduction of, or embedding of, new facts.

So the activities that are freer and more playful in nature I use when participants may already have most of the 'facts' available, and need to build upon that knowledge to create new understanding, often as part of a group consensus. There are elements of both within all the activities I have described, but the choice is simply which to bring to the front, which to prioritise, when creating new learning activities. As I've stated before, however, don't be afraid to allow the "play" to come to the front in any game you use, as this can enable the greatest benefits to emerge.

Permission to play

Playing in public, or in particular, being seen to play in public, is a political act for adults (Koh, 2014; De Koven, 2014, p. 160). Outside socially mandated acceptable modes and arenas of play (such as playing for a sports team, belonging to an amateur dramatics society, etc.), play tends to be seen as socially unacceptable for adults, reducing the amount of play they undertake, particularly free or imaginative play (Van Leet & Feeney, 2015).

This can be explained using Goffman's (1986) idea of sociological frames. Goffman (1971, p. 28) describes how individuals tend to play a part in any situation, asking them to 'believe that the character they see, actually possesses the attributes he appears to possess'. He talks a great deal about play, including listing nine things that must be sustained to "transform serious, real action into something playful" (Goffman, 1986, p. 41). Most importantly, he describes how keys, or keying (conventions by which an activity is perceived by participants) allow a group to decide whether or not a certain activity is play. The "frame" in which we see an activity is controlled by the internal and external prompts that affect how we react to it.

For instance, if we walk into a lecture theatre with fixed tiered seating, and see someone at the front with slides ready, we are likely to see it through a frame akin to a Victorian, didactic mode of teaching. We expect to sit still and silent for a set amount of time and be fed information from the expert at the front. Creativity and conversation will seem alien to the frame, clashing with the behaviour that the group would expect from each other in that situation. To act differently to the norms of expected behaviour in any situation causes "embarrassment" (Goffman, 1967) to both the non-conformer and those around them.

Members of any group naturally signal to each other when they move into a play situation (Glenn et al, 1987), and a combination of this informal signalling and contextual signalling is required to enable a playful frame for learning.

Deterling (2017) uses Goffman's frames to suggest that people need 'alibis' to play, to give excuses for behaving differently to how a normative frame might suggest in a particular situation, as well as keyings (see above) that can help move the frame appropriately. He suggests that if we remove the potential for disapproving observers (Audience management); interrupt the ability for players and observers to watch each other (Awareness management); and encouraging participants to distance themselves from the play through parody or mocking the play, even while taking part (Role distancing).

For us to give people permission to play, and to enable them to give themselves that permission, we need to find ways of giving these 'alibis" for play and to 'key' play in as many ways of possible to show that it is an acceptable way of behaving.

Many of the ideas within this short book will help signal that play is acceptable, but are not enough on their own. We can't just drop a game or play type activity into more didactic style teaching and expect people to play. Instead we need to find ways of signalling that play is acceptable right from the start of any time with our learners so that they don't feel 'embarrassed' by the playful activity.

Example of games

A few examples of games and playful activities follow, please use them as inspiration to create your own games, or feel free to adapt these to suit your own practice. This includes creating your own versions based on the files where I provide links to them. If you adapt one of the games, please cite the original game somewhere in your new game (in the rules may be a sensible place?), either as a full citation to the downloadable file, or simply a reference to where you discovered it in this book.

CRAAP dice

The Challenge:	Evaluating sources of information
Number of Players:	Up to 4 per game, though many games can go on in the same room.
Time for Activity:	15-20 minutes.
Resources Required:	A CRAAP worksheet or dice (see below). An article, book chapter, or other source of information to be evaluated. Sticky notes or flipchart paper & pens.
Outline of Game:	• Each group of 3 or 4 people have a dice (see image below) and a relevant piece of information to evaluate. • They take turns in throwing the CRAAP dice. • Whichever face is uppermost (summary face is "throw again"), they use an aspect on that face to analyse the piece of information they have been given. This is noted either on a sticky note or the flipchart paper. • After 10 minutes, each group has to sum up their evaluation of the information source for the rest of the class. • Each group can then vote on the "best" analysis (without voting for themselves).

Additional Resources found at:	Printable file at: http://goo.gl/xfYHhG

This is less of a formal game and more on the "playful" end of the play – game spectrum, this is an attempt to bring playfulness into an otherwise dry exercise. The voting for the "best" analysis also brings an element of competition to help the groups focus.

This can also be done with a standard worksheet, of which there are many versions freely available online, though it loses much of the playfulness this way. The "dice" can be printed on A4 card, though it is a little fiddly to put together at that size – if you can use A3 card it is much easier!

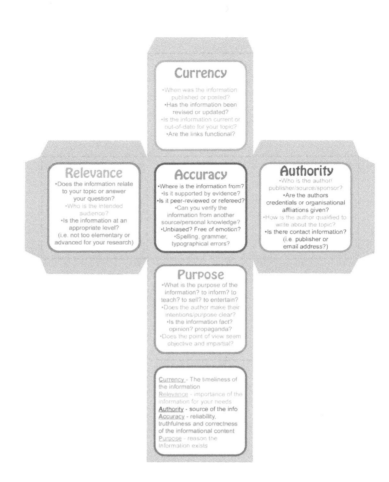

Image: The CRAAP criteria as cardboard die.

Database matching game

The Challenge:	Introducing a wide range of specialist resources to students.
Number of Players:	Between 2 and 6 per game, though many games can go on in the same room.
Time for Activity:	5 minutes, varies depending on number of cards.
Resources Required:	2 cards per group for each resource you want your students to be aware of, so these will vary according to your library and subject area. One card has the name of a resource & preferably a symbol / logo that represents it. The other card has a brief abstract describing. Stopwatch.
Outline of Game:	• Split the class into small groups. • Each group has a full set of cards. • Each groups must work together to match the name of a resource with its abstract. • Start your stopwatch, & each group must then put the cards into matching pairs. • When each group finishes they stand up and you note the time they finished. • When all groups have finished, move through the room checking if their "pairs" is correct - for each incorrect pair, they receive a time penalty of 20 seconds. The group with the fastest time (including penalties) wins!
Additional Resources	Not applicable.

Note – if you have more than a few groups, you may have to trust one person on each table to time themselves with stopwatches, instead of you keeping track of the time. Make them stand up still, as this makes it more difficult to cheat!

This game is about exposing students to the wealth of resources available for them to explore. It also forces them to consider what is behind the "name" of a resource – what would they find when they searched it?

You can vary how easy the abstracts are to match up with resources to match your class as well. A simple description might suit many classes, but something than describes the attributes rather than the content may be harder (potentially describing more than one resource) than more detailed descriptions. So "Contains brief details of potentially academic sources, though may link to the full text. Is an easy way to do citation searching" AND "A search engine from Google than attempts to search academic sources" are both descriptions of Google Scholar, but the first will probably take more discussion! So pitch your descriptions depending on what you want your class to think about and how difficult you want to make it.

I'd recommend the game then leads into a discussion about these resources – which were new to people? Did they recognise the resources easily from the descriptions, or where they surprised by some of them? What resources did people currently find useful? Would they try anything new from the ones described?

Escape rooms (in a box)

I mentioned escape rooms elsewhere in this book. I've used them a few times, including for evaluating information, bits of referencing, and other information skills. Here I discuss briefly how we can use them and offer a practical example of one I used for some inductions fairly recently. Please don't try and copy it, but instead use it as inspiration for your own escape room style games. See later in this book for guidance on how to create your own.

This particular escape room style game was for a library induction and used a dedicated box with multiple components. Any boxes that could be fitted with padlocks would do, don't feel like you need a dedicated box!

It was aimed at small groups of students doing library inductions, particularly international students and took roughly 30 minutes to complete.

The box contained 5 different puzzles, along with materials about the library, which were worked through in a linear manner. Clues were available to control how long the groups took, making sure that they could be completed in 30 minutes.

Throughout the activity, a fairly lightweight story unfolded about "evil librarians" trying to take over the library. The players had to defeat them by completely the box before these evil librarians returned to stop them!

The box in operation

The puzzles are shown over the next few pages.

Puzzle 1 was on the outside of the box and set up the initial story. The puzzle itself was hidden on the rear of the card shown below, using ink that only showed up in UV light. The reason it says "you need to keep an eye on the **time**", is because the UV torch was hidden in a clock propped against the box of puzzles.

The hidden puzzle asked:

a)   How many items an Undergraduate can borrow * Floor where the DVDs are

b)   How many items a Postgraduate can borrow / Floor where you take out books

c)   Where the reservation shelf is

Materials around the box would give the answers to these! The 3 numbers opened a 3 digit padlock to reveal puzzle 2.

Puzzle 2 was a jigsaw. When assembled, students were expected to find a floor map amongst the materials around the box and realise that the floor numbers revealed a 4 digit code for another padlock.

Puzzle 3 told some more story about the evil librarians' plans. There was also a template hidden in the box (an acetate sheet with areas blocked out using marker pen). Once the template was placed over this puzzle, it revealed some hidden questions:

(Paragraph 1) number of digits username

(Paragraph 2) print cost black and white

(Paragraph 3) minimum space student drive K

Again, the materials that were available with the box would tell them how many digits were in a student username, the print costs, and the space they had on their "K drive". This opened another 3 digit padlock.

Puzzle 4 contained some fairly simple questions, but they needed to work out how these answers fitted within a grid pattern to give a special code word. This opened a "cryptex" (it looks like the grid shown under this puzzle below!) which contained a key to the next padlock and clue).

Puzzle 5 finished off the escape room. It was a coded question asking our normal opening hours but using British Sign Language finger spelling. If they turned the answer into a 3 digit code (247 for 24 hours a day, all week long), they opened the last compartment for a congratulatory message and a prize (a badge and sweets).

As an idea, this activity worked amazingly well for small quantities of people. The self-contained nature of the box (with a few materials leant against it), meant they were quickly into the "magic circle" of play. The players felt that they had stepped into a different world and were confident in manipulating the materials and seeking out answers to the questions set.

ESCAPE ROOM induction @hudlib

Clue 1

Welcome to your library induction. You'll need to keep an eye on the **time** to reveal the first task and take a look at this clue from a different angle, to make sure you escape the induction.

There are several puzzles to solve, each one will give you access to a locked container and lead onto the next puzzle. The final puzzle will give you a prize, you can then leave the room!

You've been locked in the room by the evil rebel librarians - they want to make sure no-one learns how to use the library for their studies. They've tried long talks in induction week, specially designed to send students to sleep and deter them from using the library, but students keep coming in! This year the evil librarians have stepped up their game and locked you away to prevent you from using their resources. The only way to escape is to solve the puzzles and to learn the basics of how to use the library.

There is a rumour that the good librarians are winning the fight against the evil rebel librarians - so if you need an extra clue, one may be able to help out...

ESCAPE ROOM ^{induction} @hudlib

Clue 3

We need to deter a higher number of students from using the library, accessing our precious articles, wearing out the books with their sticky digits, and recklessly logging onto Summon with their usernames and passwords all day and night from home and on campus.

We've tried print signs to keep them out, and barricading the door comes at too high a cost to us - there are only so many of us that can do it. It is clear now, in black and white, we need to get rid of the other librarians, the helpful ones, who encourage such wanton use of our library.

As a minimum we need to find space to herd the other library staff into. The student population will never know, we will drive them into the hidden level 1 of the building. WE STRIKE TONIGHT!

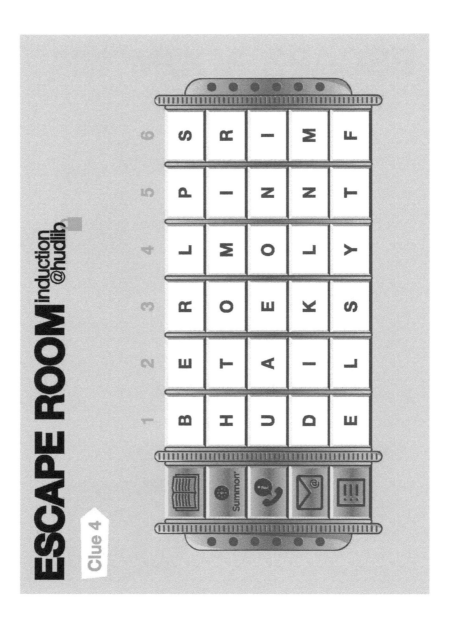

40

ESCAPE ROOM induction @hudlib

You can borrow most books from the Library for:

1. You can't borrow them!
2. 1 day
3. 1 week
4. 2 weeks
5. As long as you want
6. Until someone else requests them

ESCAPE ROOM ^{induction}@hudlib

Your Unimail email also comes with:

1. Access to Office 365 apps like Word
2. Access to Google Apps
3. A free Dropbox account
4. Some free computer games to download
5. Unlimited storage space
6. Someone to answer your emails for you

ESCAPE ROOM induction @hudlib

Clue 4

The 24 hour IT helpline number is:

1. 01484 473737
2. 01484 472052
3. 01484 422288
4. 01484 484100
5. 01484 472093
6. 01484 473888

ESCAPE ROOM induction @hudlib

Your reading lists are normally accessed through UniLearn. They give you:

1. Lists of people who can read and summarise books for you

2. Collections of books you'll need to buy before starting your studies

3. Everything you'll need to read whilst at university

4. Information on some key materials to read at university, set by your lecturer

5. Recommendations by the Library of the latest books on your subject area

6. The best snacks to eat while reading Library books

ESCAPE ROOM induction @hudlib

Summon is the Library search engine for finding:

1. Which computers are free
2. Print and electronic books, journal articles and newspaper articles
3. Print resources (such as books and articles) only
4. Online materials (such as books and articles) only
5. The best place to eat out nearby
6. Your timetable

ESCAPE ROOM ^{induction}
@hudlib

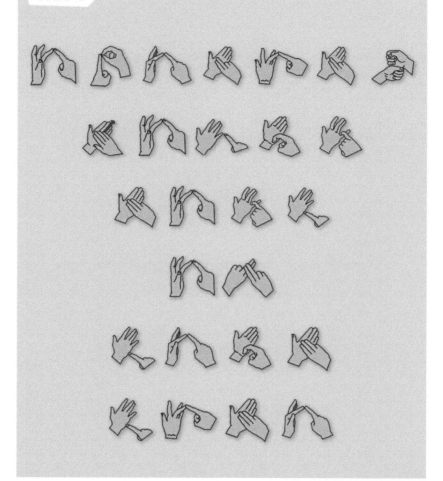

46

ESCAPE ROOM induction @hudlib

Congratulations!

You have defeated the evil librarians who wanted to keep you from learning about the Library. You now have all the basic information to start using the Library and you will find only the good librarians from now on.

Take a badge from this last box to show how well you did!

Fake or Fab

The Challenge:	Encourage people to evaluate conferences and decide whether they are high quality, or even completely fake conferences.
Number of Players:	Multiple groups of up to 4 in each group. Can have as many groups as you wish running at any time.
Time for Activity:	30-40 minutes activity. 10 minute discussion.
Resources Required:	A set of question cards. Some online access for at least 1 person per group. A recent "call for papers" from a conference.
Outline of Game:	• Give each group a printout of a conference call for papers. These can be a mixture of ones you know are high quality, along with those that may be more predatory. • The group can pick 2 questions from each category to try and answer in a time limit. • At the end they have to persuade the rest of the room whether or not their conference is Fab (worth going to!), or Fake (not worth it!).
Additional Resources found at:	See blog posts at: https://gamesforlibraries.blogspot.com/search/label/predatory Think, Check, Attend may also be of use: https://thinkcheckattend.org/

I receive multiple emails a week from conferences inviting me to submit papers. Some of these are obviously dodgy in some way, others I *know* are high quality through personal experience or recommendation. Fairly recently, however, I was intrigued by one that looked really interesting, but I couldn't be sure whether it was a genuinely high quality conference, or something that wouldn't be worth my time going to.

At the same time I noticed an increase in the number of researchers (particularly early career academics) asking about conferences at our enquiry desk at the University of Huddersfield.

This game is my attempt to wrap some questions we should ask about conferences into a game in a way that enables discussion and a nuanced decision making, rather than a "tick box" style approach to assessing them.

No matter what the conference is, the groups normally end up with a set of positives and negative points about it, but also a clear view about the overall quality.

It can really help researchers realise that they often can't tell at first glance which conferences are worth their time and limited budgets to go to. They tend to leave with a more nuanced view of conference calls and a set of questions to consider before applying for one.

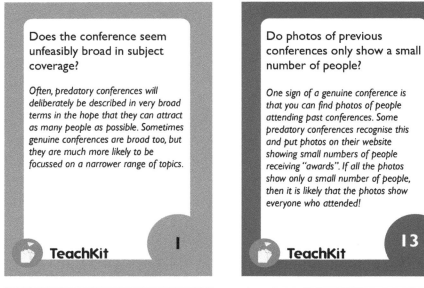

Does the conference seem unfeasibly broad in subject coverage?

Often, predatory conferences will deliberately be described in very broad terms in the hope that they can attract as many people as possible. Sometimes genuine conferences are broad too, but they are much more likely to be focussed on a narrower range of topics.

TeachKit

1

Do photos of previous conferences only show a small number of people?

One sign of a genuine conference is that you can find photos of people attending past conferences. Some predatory conferences recognise this and put photos on their website showing small numbers of people receiving "awards". If all the photos show only a small number of people, then it is likely that the photos show everyone who attended!

TeachKit

13

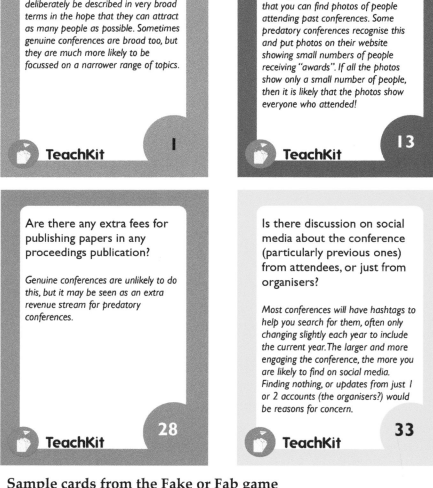

Are there any extra fees for publishing papers in any proceedings publication?

Genuine conferences are unlikely to do this, but it may be seen as an extra revenue stream for predatory conferences.

TeachKit

28

Is there discussion on social media about the conference (particularly previous ones) from attendees, or just from organisers?

Most conferences will have hashtags to help you search for them, often only changing slightly each year to include the current year. The larger and more engaging the conference, the more you are likely to find on social media. Finding nothing, or updates from just 1 or 2 accounts (the organisers?) would be reasons for concern.

TeachKit

33

Sample cards from the Fake or Fab game

Journal analysis through collage

The Challenge:	Extracting useful information from a journal article.
Number of Players:	Small groups of 3 or 4 learners, the main limit on number of groups is the space required for cutting and pasting.
Time for Activity:	15 – 25 minutes.
Resources Required:	A copy of a journal article per group. Scissors, glue, pens and flipchart paper.
Outline of Game:	• Each group receives a copy of a journal article, some scissors, glue sticks, and a piece of flip chart paper containing a template representing a house. • They are then tasked with cutting elements (words, phrases and sentences) out of the article that address certain key areas and to stick them onto the template appropriately. • They can write a few words on the template at the end summing up what they have found.
Additional Resources found at:	Not applicable.

Analysing a journal article and extracting relevant information to re-use in your own work, is a higher level information literacy skill than students new to university may be used to. Often undergraduate students, plus some international postgraduate students, will be used to scanning material and cutting and pasting that material into their own work. If lessons on plagiarism and referencing have been successful, they may know to reference that material correctly, including paraphrasing appropriately, but the earlier act of critically reading, evaluating, and extracting information from a source may be difficult or alien to them.

Rather than use a highly structured, formal game to help students gain these skills, I've instead made it a more creative and playful activity. I've tried to engineer a learning situation where students can think with their hands, and can physically cut and paste elements from one information source (such as a journal article) into a useful summary for that article. I've tried different shapes and structures for this, but the example given here is one I created with a colleague to use with Education students as part of an academic intervention project.

Students cut elements (words, phrases and sentences) out of the chosen article that address the following areas and to stick them onto the template appropriately.

1) The main purpose of the article (why has the author chosen to write this article?) (main body of the house)
2) The key question the author is addressing in this article (front door)
3) What facts or data the author has used to support any conclusions made (foundations)
4) The main conclusions in the article (roof)

5) The key concepts or theories in the article (windows)
6) Any underlying assumptions underpinning the author's thinking (what are they taking for granted?) (Bricks)
7) How can it be applied to your assignment/project (chimney pot)

They then write one or two sentences in their own words to sum up each of the sections of their collage. They stick their collages to the wall of the classroom and spend time looking at each other's work, adding a few notes (if they wish) to other collages. This activity finishes with a short reflection by every group that is fed back to the whole class. The ability to "think with their hands" in cutting and organising the elements before summarising them helps the thought process of students and helps them see how they can pull information out of a long, serious journal article with confidence in future.

The library story (A to Z cards)

The Challenge:	Encourage students to consider the range of services found in your library. Ideal as part of an induction.
Number of Players:	Groups of up to 8. I've done this in a room of about 50 people, split into smaller groups.
Time for Activity:	10-15 minutes activity. 10 minute discussion.
Resources Required:	A set of cards with images that represent library services (enough for 2 or 3 per person). These can be photos from your library, more generic images representing services, or the A to Z cards linked to below.
Outline of Game:	• Deal all the cards within a group. • The first player starts with "I went to the library and I…" continued with an example of what they did based on one of their cards. • Then the next player continues the same story, extending it with one of their own cards / services. • Every time a player forgets the sequence before them, they get a point. • The player(s) with the least points win!
Additional Resources found at:	http://libraryAtoZ.org

This game uses the ideas of visual prompts for learners and some fairly lightweight narrative or storytelling that helps them remember the content of the session more effectively. It is the same as the game I used to play as a child called "I went to the market..." where we would work our way through the alphabet, but extended by the use of the visual prompts.

As well as introducing the services they may be able to use in your library, it can also flag up services that you don't have, but may be expected.

A more involved version would be to have each person draw a small number of cards from the pack (4 or 5) and construct a small story detailing what they did in an imaginary visit to the library, based on the cards drawn. Points can be given by the other members of the group based on originality, humour, and knowledge of the library.

Model making and Lego

The Challenge:	Reflecting on a partly completed literature review and finding ways to improve it.
Number of Players:	Up to 20.
Time for Activity:	At least an hour. Varies according to number of students who need to feedback.
Resources Required:	An assortment of Lego pieces.
Outline of Game:	• 5 minutes working individually to build a metaphor for their literature review from Lego. • Explain this model to the group. • Then spend 10 minutes working together in groups to build their "ideal" literature review. • Switch again to individual model building to create their own action plan to improve their literature review.
Additional Resources found at:	This is based upon (though not strictly following) the Lego Serious Play Methodology: http://seriousplaypro.com/docs/LSP_Open_Source_Brochure.pdf

Alongside collage activities, such as the one described above, an other creative and playful approach, rather than a structured game activity, is that of model making.

I've used modelling clay for similar activities in the past, but the example described below, making a Lego Literature Review is my favourite model making activity for information literacy skill development.

This type of activity allows learners to think with their hands, rather than just their heads, and the easy to connect nature of Lego means that it is quick and simple to build models as metaphors for the ideas I want students to express. It is inspired by the Lego Serious Play methodology, described later on in this report. When I've asked groups of students in the past how they are managing with literature reviews, the most common answer is "okay"… this approach is intended to get something a bit more meaningful from them, help them reflect, and let them build their own solutions to improve their work.

In the workshops, students each have access to a wide variety of Lego pieces, and sit in fairly small groups, though much of their work is carried out individually. They will either be final year undergraduates, or postgraduates working towards a dissertation or thesis. The activity is designed to draw out problems with their literature review while it is a work in progress and help them find solutions to improve that literature review.

Images: Lego model making in action

The students are given 5 minutes to build a Lego model of their literature review as it is at present. The time given is deliberately short, as we don't want a too detailed model, simply a model that represents in some way the literature review that they can then talk about. The act of building the model physically with their hands helps them reflect and think about their literature review in a different way and they can then talk about the model as one step removed from themselves, making it 'safer' to express their progress and problems.

Once the 5 minutes is up, they then have to explain their model to the rest of their group (if a small class, this is to the whole class, otherwise to the small number of people they are sat with). In itself, this enables much richer reflection and sharing than without the model making activity.

The next step is to spend 10 minutes working as a group to build their vision of an "ideal" literature review. This is shared with the whole class and discussion held around the similarities and variances between the models to get a whole group vision of what an ideal literature review would look like and how that may be achievable (with the instructor facilitating that discussion). The result should be a list of characteristics of a good literature review and an idea of how to achieve it.

The learners can then return to their original, individual models and build their own solutions showing what they need to do next to turn their existing literature review into an 'ideal' one. They share that with the rest of their group, which becomes their action plan to carry out after the session.

Please be aware that some students can find building metaphorical models, explaining them, and even using Lego itself can be intimidating for some students. Because of this, I will normally "build up" towards a model making activity like this, with other warm up model making activities. Unless you already use other similar creative techniques, I'd recommend attending a session from a skilled Lego facilitator before you try this yourself.

The playful induction

The Challenge:	Make library inductions more engaging and help students retain some basic facts.
Number of Players:	I did this with up to 200 in a lecture theatre!
Time for Activity:	20 minutes (10 minute crossword, 10 minute discussion)
Resources Required:	A printed crossword and library leaflet per student.
Outline of Game:	• I provided crosswords to each induction group of students, with the answers matching all the key facts we were required to cover. • The questions were 'simple' crossword type (no cryptic questions!) such as anagrams, fill in the gap, and straightforward question / answer combinations. All the answers could be found in the accompanying library guide we gave out in all inductions. • Students work in pairs (or threes at most) to complete the crosswords and offered token prizes of sweets or chocolate to the first few groups to complete the crossword in each induction.
Additional Resources found at:	Various online crossword makers available.

Inductions are always a struggle to make more engaging. Using crosswords was my first lightweight entry point into using games, and was an easy first step towards increasing engagement and helping students to remember more of the key facts from inductions.

This activity typically took around 10 minutes for the majority of groups to complete the crossword. The second half of the session was then spent with the answers displayed on screen at the front of the class, while we discussed the answers as a class. This was the key to its success as a learning tool, as it provided a route to check understanding of the participants and to expand on the bare facts and figures covered in the crossword in such a way that was adaptable for each class, covering the issues raised by them in the short class discussion. For smaller class sizes, it often allowed fears and concerns about using library resources to be raised and addressed in a way that was rarely managed in a standard induction.

There are plenty of free crossword generators online, especially on teaching resource websites.

These days I tend not to use crosswords, but instead use polling software like Polleverywhere[11] or Kahoot![12] and have students answers questions one at a time using their phones or other devices via text message or online.

---

[11] www.polleverywhere.com

[12] https://kahoot.it

Referencing games

The Challenge:	Help students see patterns in our standard referencing system and improve confidence.
Number of Players:	I've run this for up to 50 students, split into groups of 2 or 3.
Time for Activity:	15 mins (5 minute game, 10 minute discussion)
Resources Required:	Set of cards, each of which has a component of a reference printed on it. An APA 6th referencing guide.
Outline of Game:	• Students build the components of a reference using the elements contained on the cards. • This is done in competition with other groups in the class, with a prize for the highest scorers.
Additional Resources found at:	http://eprints.hud.ac.uk/id/eprint/25335 Includes a full set of "reference element" cards – the size suits printing on "minicards" at moo.com, or they can be manipulated for printing however you wish.

One of the areas that seems to concern students (and often staff) at all levels is referencing. Instead of worrying about *what* to reference, which should be the hardest part of referencing, they worry about the *technicalities* of *how* to reference. Even experienced academics get stressed about the exact placements of full stops, or which elements of a reference should be in italics.

Students new to a referencing style will often lack confidence, even postgraduates who have used similar styles in the past. This may not always have been helped by the typical approach to teaching referencing, which understandably tends to focus on areas like correct punctuation (for a particular style) that students can struggle with.

My approach over recent years to teaching students how to reference has been to use a simple referencing game, where students will build references using elements already laid out on cards. I use these cards in a few different ways depending on the group, but most typically in the way describe below.

Images: some example referencing cards.

I split the class into small groups, preferably pairs or threes. Each group has access to a large number of cards with referencing elements printed upon them (such as Author, Date, Place of publication, etc.). They can then pick what type of reference they want to build first depending on how difficult a reference they want to try and how many points they will try to earn. I vary this by class but I often give 1 point for a book reference, building up to 5 points or the most difficult (normally a conference proceeding), so they choose their own balance of difficulty versus potential number of points.

Each group has a copy of our referencing guide to help them. They have a fixed amount of time (often just 5 minutes) to earn as many points as possible through building references. I award a small prize (such as sweets or chocolate) to the group who has earned the most points, and the group who have built the most references (recognising the weaker students who may only be confident in trying the simpler references).

The game, described above, allows students to practice building references without worrying about factors such as punctuation, which are included by default on the cards. The second step is to facilitate a discussion where the groups look for patterns in the references. With several references in front of them, they start to construct rules themselves about the referencing standard, including the formatting and punctuation that many students tend to worry about. After a short discussion a group will typically have enough rules to construct a reference type that we haven't practiced as part of the game. The game and subsequent discussion allows them to practice building references using our guides, but also to *understand* how a reference is constructed and apply it to new situations, rather than focussing on remembering the exact formatting and punctuation that they apply in each situation.

A variation I use with smaller groups is to put a set of the components required to build a particular reference type in an envelope. I'll create a series of these envelopes labelled appropriately (book, journal article, website, etc.) along with the number of points on offer as above.

Each group must then complete a reference using all the components in an envelope before asking for the next, for which they have a choice of difficulty and points on offer. We can then add up the points on their envelopes to find the winner. This method is more controlled than the first example, but is more time consuming to set up and more difficult to control in larger groups.

Referencing mix and match

The Challenge:	Revising the basic rules of building a reference.
Number of Players:	As many as you want. This referencing game can work well in a large lecture theatre.
Time for Activity:	5-10 minutes.
Resources Required:	A4 cards, each of which contains an element of a reference (Author, date, etc.)
Outline of Game:	• Invite people to the front of the class and give them an element of a reference each, asking them to hold it in front of them (visible to the room). • They should then shuffle around until the reference is in the correct order, with help from the rest of the class. • Start with "easy" reference types, then build up towards harder types that require more thought! • When the reference is "correct", the components can be stuck to the wall somewhere visible to everyone in the class. The "volunteers" at the front can be replaced by other volunteers for the next reference.
Additional Resources found at:	Not applicable

I saw a variation of this presented at LILAC[13] in 2018, where the presenters used balloons instead of cards.

A relatively easy version of this would include punctuation on the cards in the correct position. To make it harder, put the punctuation on separate cards, so they have to put full stops, etc., in the correct position too.

You can also do this on a screen at the front of the class (an interactive whiteboard is good for this), asking people to drag elements of a reference into the correct position on the screen.

_____

[13] https://www.lilacconference.com

SEEK!

The Challenge:	Get students to understand how to construct a search strategy and why it might be useful to do so.
Number of Players:	Between 4 & 8 per game. I typically use this in classes of around 30 students, with 5 or 6 games going on at the same time. Largest class I've done this with was just over 60 (about 12 games running!).
Time for Activity:	20 minutes (10 minute game, 10 minute discussion)
Resources Required:	SEEK! cards, plus sweets or counters for keeping score.
Outline of Game:	<ul><li>Players have 2 cards each.</li><li>On each players turn they can choose which of their cards to play, asking a question to another player of their choosing. They then discard this card and draw another.</li><li>Wildcards are included to add a random element to the game, which also give positive messages about using library services.</li></ul>
Additional Resources found at:	http://eprints.hud.ac.uk/19345/ Includes the full game, player and teacher instructions, plus editable question cards.

One area I have struggled to teach in a way that was meaningful to students at any level, has been how to construct a search strategy. Often students and staff will struggle to express their information needs in a way that will give relevant and useful results in a search engine, that is to create a sensible and effective search strategy. Over the years I have lectured, given various worksheets, and even shown videos of plastic dinosaurs helping a student to search[14], but while they all had limited effect, few seemed to reflect on the subject matter and realise it was a skill that would make a valuable difference to their own practice. As my interest in using games for developed, I saw this as a prime candidate for a game.

The game questions cover topics related to picking keywords from an assignment question and combining those terms in a typical search engine. Most questions are relatively straightforward, but some are deliberately left open to interpretation to encourage discussion.

Images: Some example SEEK! question cards

The game was designed to introduce the same ideas of constructing a search strategy that I have covered in various

[14]http://www.library.usyd.edu.au/skills/elearning/learn/topic/index.php

ways in the past. However, it put the focus on the students to reflect on the knowledge they already had and apply it to the game. Similar questions were asked repeatedly in the game, allowing students to develop that knowledge themselves (whether asking questions or answering them), rather than me presenting them with the 'answer' from the front of the class. The game allowed differentiation, with the mix of questions challenging all levels of students and a wildcard factor balancing the game so that lower ability students still had a chance of winning. In addition, as made clear in the teacher's instructions, there is another layer of learning after the game itself. After the 10 minute game, we spend roughly 10 minutes discussing the game, particularly the trickier or more ambiguous questions. This reinforces the learning that takes place in the game, and helps the whole group reflect on the questions covered and what it may mean for their own academic or professional practice.

The full rules, including instructions for the teacher, are available to download.[15]

There is also a newer version of SEEK with a revised format and updated questions. This isn't currently available as an open educational resource, but professionally printed cards can be bought.[16]

> SEEK!
>
> What are the most relevant terms in this research question?
>
> "What impacts do tuition fees have on university students in the UK?"
>
> If you wish, cover the lower half of this card and show it to the other player.
>
> Answer: "tuition fees";"university students", and "UK".

Image: An updated SEEK! question card

---

[15] http://eprints.hud.ac.uk/19345/
[16] https://teachkit.org.uk/shop/

70

SOURCES

The Challenge:	Raising awareness of and issues around using a range of information sources. Illustrates that different assignments may require different mixes of sources.
Number of Players:	Between 2 and 6 per game, though many games can go on in the same room.
Time for Activity:	10 minutes for a round of the game, followed by around 10 minutes discussion.
Resources Required:	SOURCES cards – downloadable from the link below.
Outline of Game:	<ul><li>Each player is dealt 2 "assignment" cards and 4 "resource" cards.</li><li>The aim is to collect sets of resources to match the requirements on their "assignment" cards.</li><li>Each turn the current player can swap an "assignment" card, or draw a card from the resource stack.</li><li>After drawing, if the player wishes, they can put a set down in front of them, earning the points indicated on the assignment card, & draw a replacement assignment card until no more are left.</li><li>When any player has used all their assignment cards and there are no fresh ones to draw the game ends.</li></ul>

Additional Resources	Full game and additional files available at http://eprints.hud.ac.uk/19346/

This game is a mixture of exposing learners to some basic characteristics of information sources and some of the issues around finding and using a range of information sources. It is a set collection card game, where the sets vary according to the "assignment cards". The learners can balance whether to try to earn high points by collecting towards the more difficult assignments, or low points by going for easy ones.

The "resource" cards give an outline of several information sources, including books, academic journals, and newspapers. The balance of cards in the deck are such that it is easy to collect low quality resources and harder to find the higher quality ones – so there are lots of "general websites", but fewer "academic journal articles". So if the players want to earn the highest points, they have to spend longer trying to collect the scarce resources.

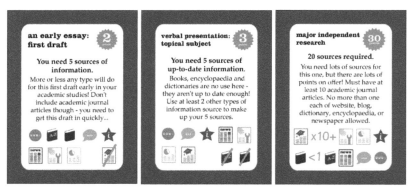

Images: Sample SOURCES "assignment" cards.

Once the game has been played, it leads into a group discussion. The exact topics will depend on your groups and the key learning objectives you want them to take away, but good general questions are:

• Did you find some resources easier to find than others? Do you think this reflects "real life"?

• What sort of information sources do you think might be useful for your next assignment? Has your opinion changed after playing the game?

• Who got a wildcard? What was it and why do you think your wildcard gave you points or penalised you? Does that reflect the real search experiences of the group?

• What "specialist" resources do you think apply to your subject areas? Could you think of any examples?

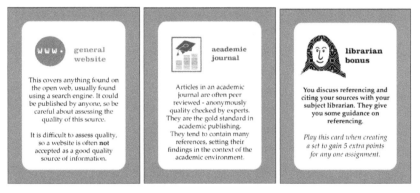

Images: Sample SOURCES "resource" cards, including a bonus card

Sources of Information Cards

The Challenge:	Extracting key information from a source of information and storing it for later
Number of Players:	Individual activity – no limit to number of people doing it at any one time.
Time for Activity:	10-15 minutes.
Resources Required:	A sample source of information per person. A4 or A5 card, scissors, glue and pens.
Outline of Game:	• Learners should be encouraged to scan through the article in just a few minutes – so speed read, not reading in detail! • Then they should fold the card into half (so it looks like a greeting card). • On the front they should draw an image or write a few words that sum up what the article is about. • They should cut out important or useful phrases from the source of information and glue them to the inside. They might also find it useful to write a few words to sum things up too! • On the back of the card, they can cut and paste the bibliographic elements they need to create a reference. • The whole greetings card becomes a short summary of that source of information.

	• If they try this for multiple sources, it creates a bank of information they can dip into without needing to return to the original source.
Additional Resources found at:	Not applicable

If you wish, this can be extended into a referencing activity. Bring some string and pegs and get the learners to hang up their cards in the order they would appear in their reference lists. This may also inspire them to use the activity afterwards, as a set of cards hanging up near their desks can act as a visual summary of the sources they may wish to use.

A small variation is to create postcards, with a summary of the information (including pasted elements on one side) and on the other, bibliographic information (the address!) and a few key words that sum up that information source.

Top Resources

The Challenge:	Introducing the range of resources available through the library and promoting them.
Number of Players:	Between 2 and 5 per game, though many games can go on in the same room.
Time for Activity:	10 minutes
Resources Required:	1 deck of 30-50 Top Resources cards for each group of 5.
Outline of Game:	Top Resources is a card game in the style of Top Trumps. Each card highlights a library resource such as a database, journal, etc. <ul><li>Taking turns, a player chooses a category on their topmost card and calls out her "resource" and the score in that category.</li><li>The other players call out their score in that category from their topmost card.</li><li>The player with the highest score wins all the cards.</li><li>In the case of a draw, the cards are all placed in the centre and the next player to win a round, also wins these cards.</li><li>Play progresses clockwise until all only 1 player remains or a pre-agreed time limit is reached.</li></ul>
Additional Resources found at:	Example files and templates: http://goo.gl/VWjVql

The exact content of the pack of cards would vary depending on the resources each library would wish to promote, so the link given above goes to a blank template that can be filled in as required, rather than providing ready to use cards. It is recommended that the values are all out of 100. This allows similar resources to have slightly varying scores and makes gameplay easier, compared to scores out of 10.

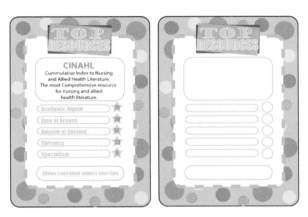

Images: An example blank card and a completed one.

The cards are templates that are designed to be adapted and have the following printed on them:

- Top Resources Logo
- Space for name of the Resource
- Academic Rigour
- Ease of Access
- Amount of Content
- Currency

- Specialism
- Space for a short text description of the resource

Ideally, print the back of the cards with a "Top Resources" logo for a more professional finish.

I'd recommend a firm time limit for this game to suit your lesson, using a timer at the front of the class, or individual timers on the tables. Otherwise this game can last a fair while! 10 minutes should be enough to run through all the cards in a pack more than once.

When the game has been played, it should lead into a 5 or 10 minute discussion. Ask questions such as:

- "What resources had you already heard about?"
- "Which resources were new to you? What do you think these new resources may be good for?"
- "Do you agree with the scores on the cards? Any you would change?"

A nice variation is to give out cards with the names of resources on, but no scores. Ask people to work in groups for a set time period to assign values to each of them. They should feedback to the whole class with their scores and justify the relative values they assign!

Example of Playful Interventions

Most of the examples in the previous section were fairly recognisable as games, or at least game like activities. This section is more "playful" interventions, that is, activities you can carry out that may bring more play into a session, or help to give your learners permission to play (See Walsh, 2018 for more on this!).

As such, they are unlikely to have specific learning outcomes in mind, beyond the generic benefits of play (e.g. team building). Instead, they help frame the situation for your learners as being one in which they are allowed to play. This will help any other learning games you use be more effective, as well as increasing engagement and interactivity in a session.

Bubbles

Where to use it:
It can work in any classroom, including large lecture theatres.

What it does:
This breaks the perception of the "expert" at the front being too serious to interact with, instead showing a playful element and echoing back to childhood play. It helps to give "permission to play" throughout the session, setting up a "playful" frame, rather than a traditional "didactic education" frame in your learners' minds.

How to do it:
The idea is incredibly simple. Using some bubble mixture and a wand, blow bubbles as people come into the room! While they carry out activities of any sort may also be an appropriate time to blow bubbles.

Variations:
Leave bubbles around the room too (you can buy multi-packs of bubble mixture in party sections of many shops). Encourage your learners to blow bubbles at the same time that you do. This goes further to encourage play as you are explicitly giving them permission to carry out a playful activity (as well as the implicit invite implied by your bubble blowing).

Chatterboxes

Where to use it:
It can work in any classroom, including large lecture theatres.
Also works as part of any handouts for outside the session.

What it does:
Provides a playful random element into an activity.
In common with many of these activities, the materials can
also echo back to childhood play, helping to give "permission
to play" throughout the session.

How to do it:
There are lots of different names for chatterboxes (fortune
teller is another common one!). They are the little folded paper
devices that can be used to randomly reveal a hidden message.

In a previous book, Emma Coonan and I (2013, pp. vii-viii)
used a chatterbox as a random "chapter chooser" – the book is
open access[17], so take a look as an example!

The hidden centre panels of a chatterbox can be used to
allocate tasks in a random manner. For example, if you use
CRAP as the criteria for evaluating a source, have one letter of
each in the centre, with a line of text explaining it.

---

[17]

http://eprints.hud.ac.uk/id/eprint/17339/7/onlyconnectprintversion.p
df

Traditionally (in my school playground!) we had colours on the outside. Someone would pick a colour and the chatterbox was moved once for every letter of that colour. They then picked a number written on one of the panels revealed – the chatterbox was moved that amount of times. Finally, they picked one of the numbers finally revealed and the panel lifted up to reveal a message. You, of course, can pick whatever you want as the items to pick each time!

There are many templates freely available online to make your own. I recommend you print them on A3 paper if possible, as it makes enough space for larger adult fingers to fit into the chatterbox!

Variations:
There are lots of playful ways of mixing up the order of an activity. To get the same benefits, it can help to pick one that your learners are likely to have encountered in playful situations. So dice (including custom dice with messages on each face, like the CRAAP dice above) can do a similar task.

If you use PowerPoint slides, you can also do something at a class wide level, using images hyperlinked to particular slides. The class can vote on which image you click on next, which then jumps to the appropriate slide. (To jump back to all the images, each put in another link, or press the number of the slide then the <enter> key!)

Learning while walking

Where to use it:
Any time you feel confident you can let your learners out of the classroom and be sure they will come back! Preferably somewhere with a pleasant outdoor space, in nice weather.

What it does:
Provides a change of scene and so helps to disrupt the frame in which they see their learning as happening. In other words, it can shift their expectations from a traditional didactic style learning environment, into one where they are able to play, be valued equally, and learn independently.

How to do it:
Whenever you have built time into your session for group discussion or reflection. Set them the same task but ask them to walk to a particular spot and back discussing it in groups. Pick the spot you want them to walk to according to the time you have for the discussion.

This works particularly well for discussing things in pairs, as one person can talk on the way out, the other on the way back.

Variations:
You can also do activities much more similar to a Psychogeographic walk by giving your learners a set of prompts to do on their walk! This would be more time consuming than the short discussion walks outlined above.

Mixing up groups (in playful ways)

Where to use it:
In any classroom where you want to mix up where people are sat, particularly for group work. I think it works brilliantly in tiered lecture theatres.

What it does:
People often sit with friends, or those they are most familiar with. It is common practice to try to mix up groups to get fresh interactions amongst people. This activity does that, but in a way that sets the "playful" scene right from the start, setting the expectation of play and interaction into your learners minds.

How to do it:
I saw Anthea Moys[18] do this at the start of a keynote talk she gave and I've used it myself since then.

Wait until everyone else is in the room, then come in as though you were late and in a massive rush. Climb over seats, ask people if you can squeeze past, and slowly disrupt as much of the room as you can manage to as you make your way to the front.

Once there, make a comment about it being a pain when people are late to the theatre or cinema and have to push passed people. Ask all your learners to pretend that they are in

---

[18] http://antheamoys.com/

that situation, and they need to move around the room looking for their seat.

When they have mixed themselves up thoroughly (it doesn't take long!), shout "STOP". Once everyone has stopped moving, tell them the show is starting, so they must be in the right places to sit down.

They will be mixed up, energised, and ready to learn in a playful way.

Variations:
There are lots of much simpler ways than the above of mixing up a class and randomly allocating them to groups. A really simple, but still playful, one is to give everyone a boiled sweet as they enter (with instructions not to eat them!). Then allocate groups by sweet colour!

Music and video

Where to use it:
It can work in any classroom, including large lecture theatres.

What it does:
Disrupt the way in which your learners feel about the space.

How to do it:
I've used music in various ways over the years, most often to "set the scene" as people come into the teaching space, but also for marking out sections of a teaching session. For example, I start music playing when we start an activity, then lower it down until silent to mark the end of that activity – the change in background noise can sometimes be more effective than verbally calling STOP to mark the end!

As part of encouraging people to see the classroom as a playful space, I'm increasingly using *silly* songs for this. YouTube can be a massive resource for these silly songs, with pieces like *Owls hate Simon Cowell* and *Kenya: Where can you see lions* by Mr Weebl[19] some of my favourites. If you trawl YouTube for songs, make sure you listen to them all the way through to make sure that they are appropriate for your learners!

_____

[19] https://www.youtube.com/user/mrweebl/videos

Paper plane feedback

Where to use it:
It can work in any classroom, including large lecture theatres.

What it does:
This continues any encouragement of playfulness right the way until the end of any teaching session. It can increase the number of feedback forms completed and returned.

How to do it
Print on A4 sheets of paper whatever questions you may wish to ask as part of collecting feedback in a session.
Instead of asking your learners to complete the feedback forms and leave them somewhere convenient as they leave, tell them to fold up their feedback forms into paper planes and throw them to the front (once completed!).
You may wish to print a paper plan template on the back to help people who may not know how to make one.

Variations:
Providing a target can also make this activity a little bit more fun. Consider providing a small prize for the first person to land their feedback plan in a container (such as paper bin) you've laid out for this purpose, or even the first person to hit you with their plane.

Pass the Parcel

Where to use it:
It can work in any classroom, including large lecture theatres.

What it does:
This is a variation of the old teaching idea of planting questions amongst your learners. The larger the class (particularly in large lecture theatres), the harder it is for anyone to ask questions, or answer them when you ask. This "breaks the ice", showing that it is ok for your learners to have their voice heard in the room. It also echoes back to childhood games for many learners, particularly in the UK. This helps to place them in a playful mindset.

How to do it:
Many of you will have played this as a children's party game. Typically a small present is wrapped up in multiple layers of wrapping paper, sometimes with a smaller gift (such as a sweet) between each layer. Music is played, and the parcel is passed around the children at the party. As the music is stopped (at random), whoever has the parcel takes off one layer of paper. The music starts again, and the parcel continues to be passed around the room.

When I do this, I typically include a question (and a small prize!) under each layer of paper. When someone removes a layer, they must read out that question, which I answer at the front. Sometimes I do this with music as one section of a session, at other times I have the parcel circulating throughout the session and the signal for removing a layer of paper is when I advance a powerpoint slide.

Variations:
I've also done something very similar with homemade Christmas crackers. Instead of them circulating around the room, I throw one at a time into the class. Whoever catches it, pulls that cracker with a neighbour and one of them must ask the question. This can sometimes feel safer for my learners, as there is always a pair of people who can agree between them who reads out the question!

The most basic version of this may be to hide prizes (and question cards) in the room. You then tell the class to search for these prizes at an appropriate time in your session.

Things to keep hands busy

Where to use it:
Primarily in rooms laid out for group working.

What it does:
The sort of materials suggested below can encourage play and creative thinking. It also helps people during problem solving or reflective activities, giving your learners an opportunity to think with their hands as well as their heads (embodied cognition).
In common with many of these activities, the materials can also echo back to childhood play, helping to give "permission to play" throughout the session.

How to do it:
Simply leave an assortment of items in the centre of each table. You may need to give your learners explicit permission to use them, though often they will start to play with the items without prompting.
Useful materials include children's modelling clay (the scent of playdoh or plasticine will often remind your learners of playing with it when younger!), building blocks such as Lego, coloured pens, paper / sticky notes, spinning toys, and sweets.

Variations:
You can dot such materials around a lecture theatre too, but it is harder to ensure that people can reach them, than when in a classroom laid out for groupworking.

Playful Challenges

Where to use it:
Anywhere, anytime… This can be run in any classroom, but also outside scheduled sessions, or even in the workplace.

What it does:
Encourages teamworking, exploration, a sense of belonging in a space, and playfulness.

How to do it:
Make up a set of cards with challenges on! These can be handwritten, printed on normal paper, or even as properly printed playing cards (which I did with the example cards shown below).

These cards can contain challenges to complete during a "normal" session (e.g. "Ask a question during the session"), or a standalone activity that your learners complete outside the formal session (e.g. "Find the highest spot on campus"). Challenge your students to complete their task, or tasks, within a set time period.

If you wish, you could set a way of "proving" that the task has been completed, such as putting photographic proof on social media, or getting a stamp or initials from someone else.

This playful activity is best completed in small groups (2 or 3 people), with each group given a number of tasks to complete within a strict time limit.

Example cards from a set used in an orientation activity at the University of Huddersfield.

Variations:
Give individual challenges in a session and ask them to conceal these challenges from their colleagues. As an extra playful step, everyone must try to guess their colleagues' challenges before the end of the session. Anyone who manages to complete their challenge without someone guessing it wins a small prize!

Creating an educational game: A process

This chapter describes the **process** I recommend people follow when creating games for their libraries. It is the same whether you create a digital or non-digital game, though I tend to recommend that initial prototypes are non-digital whatever the end format. This process is at the heart of the Making Games for Libraries workshops[20] that I run so it should be relatively simple to use this chapter as the basis of a "Making Games" workshop at your own library. If you want, use the exercises under each section to start planning your game.

We start with setting learning objectives, then consider what constraints we must work within, which game mechanics we wish to use, the style and theme of the game, then go through several rounds of prototyping and playtesting, before writing the final rules, and polishing the final game for use.

Set Learning Objectives

All games need a goal that players should be aiming for, it is one of the defining features of a game. Games you create for your library should also have an additional external goal, describing what you want the players to learn through the game. In essence, the games you will create for your library are not just for their own sake, instead you will have good reasons for creating them.

---

[20] http://gamesforlibraries.blogspot.co.uk

These reasons may be purely education, or may be related to marketing your library, but either way, consider a small number of things you want the player to learn through playing the game.

The learning objectives should be clearly stated before you start developing the game, preferably in a way that can be easily measured. They can then inform your game development, controlling the ideas or facts that you introduce to the players and the mechanisms you may use. Try to make sure you can measure whether these learning objectives have been achieved either directly through the game, or if it will be part of a class, plan how the assessment will work alongside it.

Unless you are clear about your learning objectives and how you will know if they have been met, then there is no point in planning any learning activity, including a game. Try to make sure your learning objectives are SMART (Specific, Measurable, Achievable, Realistic and Timebound) and simple to understand. For example, a learning objective for a game that says "be able to search library resources" doesn't really mean a great deal and is likely to result in a game that doesn't really meet the needs of you or your users. That could be related to constructing a search strategy, the mechanics of using your library catalogue, discovery service or databases, accessing full text of material in print or online, etc. Instead, try learning objectives like:

- By the end of the class, be able to select keywords from a typical assignment title.
- Use keywords in the library discovery service to find

ten relevant books, AV material and journal articles
before the end of the game.

These are specific, you can fairly easily measure whether they
have done them, they will hopefully be achievable and
realistic, and they are time limited.

Exercise: List two learning objectives you regularly try to get
library users to understand. Make sure they follow the
principles above.

Constraints

There are always constraints in creating games, even for major
games companies. For us in libraries, these are vital to
consider up front. There is no point in planning a game that
will need detailed staff guidance and introduction if you
already know in advance that you don't have enough staff to
cope. Don't plan a game that needs hosting on your website if
you know that getting permission (and IT staff help) to do so
involves 2 years of begging and the sacrifice of your first
born…

Instead, before you go any further, consider your key
constraints. This list of constraints may include whether the
game needs leading by an instructor, or needs to be self-
directed, it might include the amount of staff time and money
you have available to develop it, the range of skills and
knowledge players may start with and whether you have
access to particular skills sets (such as illustration, graphic
design, coding, etc.) through your staff.

These constraints should be borne in mind throughout the game development. They set the boundaries in which you can sensibly operate and help to stop you getting carried away planning something unachievable. Your constraints should help guide you towards the possible and practical for you situation.

Exercise: List 3 constraints that may be relevant to you when creating a game. This may include time, money, materials, prior skills/knowledge of the players, or anything else you see as a serious constraint on you. A frequent constraint I come across is "the game must be possible to create using whatever I can take from the stationery cabinet"!

Game mechanics

Game mechanics are those small elements of games that progress a player towards (or away from!) the goal. They are the core building blocks of any game, with the rules essentially telling the player how they fit together. They tend to be hidden slightly by the story or theme that overlays the game mechanics, but there are remarkably few of them. You should find it easy to list many of them yourself once you start to think of games in this way.

Game mechanics may include taking turns, co-operation, rolling dice (or spinners) for random chance, drawing and discarding cards, bidding, trading, collecting resources, etc., etc. I wouldn't dare try to draw up a definitive list myself (or define exactly what each means), but a quick online search will bring back examples to start off from.[21]

Rather than start off with long lists of mechanics, I recommend thinking about games you know and have played I the past. Try to write down the game mechanics from those games and then pick the ones that might suit your learning objectives and constraints.

Exercise: Think of the individual mechanics that make up some of the games you know. What 2 or 3 mechanics will you use in a game? Do these match your learning objectives and constraints well?

Style / Theme

Besides the simplest games (often of chance), most games have an overlaying narrative or theme of some sort. They engage the player with an overlying theme and look that is sometimes all that differentiates it from another game that uses the same underlying mechanics. If you can think of a consistent theme or style for your game, especially if you can include a back story at this stage, it can be easier to implement that introducing one later one and can guide your prototyping.

For example, I have two games that are almost the same in terms of game mechanics. They are both dice games at their core, where depending on the roll of dice, you either score points (which accumulate) or lose your points so far and pass the dice to the next player. The game depends on deciding

---

whether the risk of carrying on rolling outweighs the gains of banking your points so far and passing to the next player. However, one game is zombie themed – the pieces you throw represent shotguns, brains, or potential victims running away. The other game uses cute plastic pigs as dice! The themes differentiate the games and will have been core to the successful prototyping of each of them.

So consider themes that would fit in with your objectives, constraints and mechanisms. Make sure this runs throughout your prototyping.

Exercise: Will it be zombies, searching for treasure, or punk librarians? Try to choose a theme for your game, including a short "back story" if possible.

Prototyping

This is where it starts to get fun! You've gone through all the necessary, but occasionally dry steps, such as setting your learning objectives and worrying about constraints. Now you actually start to make your game!

Start off with a set of materials to make your prototype that can be obtained cheaply. Raid the stationery cupboard for sticky notes, bits of card, coloured pens, and anything else that looks interesting. Go to a "bargain" shop and see if you can find other interesting material that could fit a game. Raid old games for dice, spinners, counters, and other pieces you may be able to use.

Use these materials to try and create your first manifestation of your game. This is when your game mechanics will start to firm up. You may tweak which ones you want to use and how they will fit together to create a workable game.

Importantly, remember the decisions you have already made. The prototype should make them happen, not start again from the beginning! They constrain you and give focus to your game creation.

Don't worry about making something that looks good, with a polished feel to it, that will come at a later stage. Instead, this is about attempting to create a workable draft of the game. It can take a while, and importantly fits in a loop with the next stage, Playtesting. You should prototype and playtest as many times as is necessary to create something that works within your constraints and meets your learning objectives.

If possible, don't prototype alone, but involve other people. A group of two to four people can bounce ideas off each other and often create a better game, faster than one person on their own. That said, don't try and create a game "by committee" either – a small team is great, a large one is not recommended.

Exercise: Gather some material together and try to create a first attempt at a game. Spend between one and two hours creating your first prototype. Don't worry about getting it completely finished, just enough to get a "feel" of how the game works. Then show someone else the game who wasn't involved. Explain how it works and ask for feedback. That's your first lightweight playtest (see below) – then carry on developing it until it is at a stage where it can be "properly" playtested.

Playtesting
You've lovingly crafted your prototype. You think achieves everything you want and works well … then someone actually uses it and it all goes horribly wrong! This is what playtesting is for, it allows other to play your game and test how it actually works in practice.

When your prototype is still at a "rough and ready" stage, show it to colleagues or friends. Let them break it and point out the flaws (there will be some!). Then go back and adapt the game accordingly.

You will need to go through this process several times to work out any problems, but also to answer questions like "How long does it typically take to play?"; "Do you need more or less game pieces, questions, or points on a board?"; "How many players does the game work best with?". As the game improves, you can then try it with select groups of your end users, getting closer to the "real players" of your finished game.

The key thing is to playtest as many times as you need in order to continue improving your prototype. Only when you are towards the end of this process do you move onto the next stage, creating the rules, which will themselves need one or two rounds of playtesting.

The Rules

Initially while playtesting you can explain your game and guide the players, but will you always be able to do this? If not, you will need to have clear, easy to understand rules for the players to follow. Even if you think the players don't need rules, you may need to write some aimed at colleagues who may want to facilitate a game themselves.

Rules are difficult to write well, try to be as clear and concise as possible. Use images where appropriate, and avoid jargon. Do you have game pieces that could be confused, like more than one set of cards? If so, can you make it obvious which pieces are which, or do you need to adapt the prototype to make it easier to differentiate?

Your final rounds of playtesting should include the rules. See if the players can work out what to do without your intervention. If so, your rules will probably be okay! If not, ask what they don't understand and either adapt the rules, or adapt your prototype to make it easier to understand the rules. In addition to the obvious "how to play the game", include what pieces are required, how many players it works with, and roughly how long it should take. If your rules are aimed at an instructor rather than players, include extra information like the target group for your game, the learning objectives, and how it may fit into a broader lesson.

Exercise: If you have prototyped a game, try to write some concise rules following the guidelines above.

Run another playtest of your game and see if the players understand the rules.

Finishing the game
Your game is nearly finished, but not quite! You should have a workable game at this stage, but it will probably look a little rough around the edges. If you can polish it up, the people using it will be more likely to take it seriously. The more like a "proper" game (i.e. one you can buy in a shop) looks, the easier it will be to engage library users with it.

If you have access to graphic designers or an illustrator, this is where they can make your prototype look amazing, but you can make a difference even without these skills.

There are printers such as Game Crafter[22], SpielMateriel [23], or Ivory Graphics[24] who specialise in small print runs of custom board and card games (traditional printers want you to produce 1,000s at a time!), or business card printers that you could use for card games[25]. Just beware that depending on where you are based, customs charges may be charged, plus considerable postage fees. Just printing on higher quality materials, like proper card, can make a big difference to the look and "feel" of a card or board game.

---

[22] https://www.thegamecrafter.com

[23] http://www.spielematerial.de/en/

[24] https://gamemaker.ivory.co.uk/

[25] e.g. http://uk.moo.com/ allow a different design on each card

If you can, playtest again to make sure this final "polishing" improves the gameplay rather than detracts from it. This stage should make the rules easier to follow by differentiating between different game components more clearly, if it does the opposite then don't be afraid to go back and tweak some more. Once you've done this stage, you have a finished game! Consider sharing it under creative commons licence so other libraries can adapt and re-use your game and enjoy playing it with your library users.

If you can follow the steps above, while bearing in mind the key characteristics of games (McGonigal, 2012, *'a goal, rules, a feedback system, and voluntary participation'*), it is a relatively painless process to create a useful game activity for your teaching practice.

Creating an educational escape room style game: A process

This section is largely taken from my "Making escape rooms for educational purposes: A Workbook" (2017), which is the workbook that attendees of my escape room workshops use – the text below takes out the sections for writing elements down as you go!

Setting Learning Objectives
Remember, as in the section above, we are creating an educational experience, so like any other education intervention we should consider Learning Objectives right at the start.

For tips on aims and objectives, see the section above on making educational games.

One thing to note with escape room type activities is how you can build in differentiation. When creating your puzzles you could then either select an "easy" or "hard" version of some of the puzzles depending on the group of learners you are using the activity with, or more likely, set the puzzles towards the "hard" end of your learning objectives. You can then use appropriate hints and clues to make sure none of your learners get too frustrated, while ensuring everyone is stretched. See the **Clues and Hints** section for a little more on this idea.

Finally, before writing some learning objectives, decide on what type of learning you want to take place – one that requires prior knowledge or one that introduces all the information they need during the activity (see below).

Requires Prior Knowledge
By this, I mean that they need to know things (facts, skills, processes, etc.) about the subject you are teaching before starting the activity. The escape room activity itself will introduce little, if any, new things to learn, instead it aims to do one or more of the following:
- Test knowledge
- Apply prior knowledge to gain a deeper understanding
- Practicing skills and processes previously learnt
- Develop critical thinking skills
- Build team working skills

Learning objectives should be about application of prior knowledge and reflection on that, not learning or introducing significant amounts of new material.

No Prior Knowledge Required
This would require only "common knowledge" beforehand, rather than subject specific knowledge. It aims to do one or more of the following:
- Introduce new facts
- Introduce new processes and skills
- Develop critical thinking skills
- Build team working skills

So coming from this angle, your learning objectives would emphasise the learning of new knowledge, not the application of prior knowledge.

With this approach, you need to make sure your activity will include the access to everything they need to know to solve the puzzles!

Constraints
You should now have some learning objectives set. The next step is to think about any other constraints you need to work within. You should have a clear idea of these before you move on, they will help you focus and move forward effectively. The following list of possible constraints is not exhaustive, but covers some key constraints that most people need to consider.

These will influence heavily how your escape room activity will develop. You may wish to tweak some of your constraints later on, but do so consciously, out of choice, if you do. Don't drift accidentally into planning an activity that won't work for your situation!

Time
How long do you have for the whole activity to take place? This includes briefing players beforehand and debriefing them afterwards. Especially in educational games, the debrief could be a significant proportion of the overall time.
- How long would this leave you for the game play itself?
- Is all the time in one discrete chunk, or could some take place as an independent activity, and some as a group with you present?

Number of Players

Most importantly, how many people need to play at any one time? Also consider:

- Will it be played by small groups, or does it need to be scaled up?
- If scaled up, can you plan to have multiple streams gapping at one time in the game? Or puzzles that involve large groups? Or multiple games at the same time?
- Could it be a mixture of virtual activity and face to face, which would have different number of players at any one time as a constraint?

Amount of space available

This influences strongly the type of puzzles you can plan, as well as the dynamics and size of the groups playing the activity.

- What size is the room?
- Is it a classroom, a lecture theatre, or something else?
- Can you leave something set up in the space, or will everything need to be brought in to play?

NPCs / Gamemaster

- How much staff time do you have available to run the activity?
- Does it need to be completely standalone with an automated clue / hint system (unlikely)?
- Could you have a gamemaster (or more than one) observing and helping one or more groups?

- Or have you enough staff time available to include non player characters (NPCs), who stay present in the game?

Other

What other constraints might apply in your case?
For instance:
- You may expect to have players with differing levels of mobility, or ones with sensory impairments.
- You might not be able to stick anything to the walls, which could affect the clues and puzzles you use.
- There may be learners whose main language is different to the one your game plans to use, which might rule out certain word puzzles and puns.

Plan for these additional constraints right from the start.

Setting the Scene

You should now have some learning objectives and key constraints that will structure what you create. Another key element of this structure is how you create the world they will step into during your learning game. Will it have a strong theme, a strong narrative, both, or neither?

Strong Theme

For example, "Ancient Egypt" or "Alien Spaceship". There may not be an underlying story, but try to build a coherent "world" within this theme. Any obvious clashes with the theme and your puzzles and materials should be avoided. For instance, don't include a digital clock in a "Victorian London" theme!

A strong theme can help people feel more engaged with the activity than if it is absent. It can be easier to plan for that a strong narrative.

Strong Narrative
For example, "You have 60 minutes to defuse a bomb" or "You must escape the cell before the prison guards return", with all the puzzles sensibly progressing you along this story. Anything that is obviously tangential to this story should be avoided. You should try to create an activity where there is enough backstory and plot to draw in the players effectively. A strong narrative can be very engaging, more so than a strong theme without an associated and clear storyline.

Strong Theme and Narrative
This involves both a story and theme that are consistent and fit together well! This is harder for you to plan for, but will provide the highest levels of engagement possible. Both the theme and narrative help reinforce the magic circle of play discussed in the introduction and its associated benefits.

Weak Theme and Narrative
You might decide not to have a strong theme or narrative at all, beyond the challenge of beating the puzzles.
This might be comparatively easy to create (and move into different settings?), but will be likely to bring less of the benefits of play as an educational approach.
It also gives nowhere for "weak" puzzles to hide, so you need to very confident in your puzzles to decide to go for this approach.

Puzzle Organisation

There are multiple ways of organising your escape room activity, with a few "ideal" formats listed below. In reality, many real life escape rooms will be a hybrid mixture, but you may lean heavily towards one or the other when designing yours.

Sequential

The simplest structure, where one puzzle is discovered and must be solved at a time, with each puzzle's solution leading to the next one.

This could be hard to scale up, unless you have lots of groups doing duplicate learning games.

Parallel

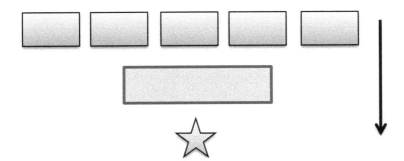

A completely open structure, where all puzzles are available to work on at the same time, leading to a "meta-puzzle" at the end, which depends on all the prior puzzles being solved. It can be hard for players to work out what to do next, or which clue is for which problem! It does, however, have good potential for scaling up, with different groups working on separate puzzles, which are then brought together at the end.

Multiple paths

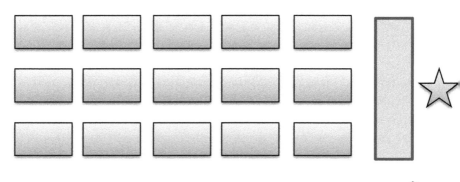

A cross between the first two, this gives multiple pathways, which lead onto a final meta-puzzle. It has potential to give a richer scaling experience, with multiple groups taking part. You could construct each path to include the same learning outcomes, then coming together just to complete the final puzzle.

Hybrid
Simply a mix of everything, and far more likely than following one simple structure in a real life room. You may start with a

simple sequence, then split into some multiple paths, and have meta-puzzles at various points in the activity.

There is no right or wrong way to organise the puzzles. Just try what makes sense to you, especially considering the difficulty of scaling up the activity.

Make sure that whatever structure you end up with, the learners can make sense of it and don't get "lost" and unsure what to do next.

When moving onto creating the puzzles (next), it can often be easiest to look at any final meta-puzzle first, then work backwards from this.

Possible Puzzles

The list of types of puzzles here is not meant to be exhaustive, but simply to prompt you to think of types of puzzles you could use when creating your own educational escape room. Look through this list briefly before going onto the next step, prototyping, then come back for ideas!

The best sources of ideas for puzzles are your own experiences though. Think about puzzles you have seen (in any context), play escape rooms and think how you might adapt puzzles you see in those rooms, and look at puzzle books like the brilliant (but out of print) "Puzzlecraft" by Selinker and Snyder (2013).

Add a Material

This isn't very often seen in escape rooms, but might have potential in educational escape rooms. Add a material to something in order to solve a puzzle.

For example:

1) Add a liquid to raise a key from the bottom of a fixed bottle.
2) Add iron filings to reveal a message written magnetically below a board.

I can't help feeling that this would suit chemistry lessons beautifully! (e.g., change the colour of a solution to act as a filter and reveal a hidden message!)

Assembly

Physically putting together objects to from something new. At its simplest, it could be a jigsaw, or add a cog or handle to a mechanism to make it work.

It's often less obvious than this though, and a nice example for educational escape rooms is to put a sheet of acetate with highlighted areas, or card with sections cut out, to reveal a hidden message on an otherwise innocent looking clue!

Ciphers

Unlike a simple substitution of one symbol / letter / number for another, these are more complicated and may include a cipher wheel (or similar) to enable you to solve it, requiring you to find the "key" to work the cipher. If you search online for "cipher wheels", there are lots of examples that can be printed off to use.

Counting

This is really simple, but really common. A clue points towards a particular item being important, and it requires you to find and count the number of those items. It could be straightforward, but if you require people to identify which items belong to a class of objects, it could make this a good one for educational escape rooms.

For example, a long list of chemicals and the clue "Acids, bases, salts" could require players to identify which chemical are which (out of acids, bases and salts!) and count them to get a 3 digit code as the answer.

Engaging with actors

This is any non-player characters present, who can be interacted with as part of the activity. They can provide extra depth to the scene, or answer set questions in response to questioning (that you would need to prepare beforehand). Having yourself as a non-player character could enable you to adapt your responses according to your learners' needs and provide in built differentiation… but you would then need to think carefully about wider tips or clues and how they would be provided without stepping out of character.

Hand to eye co-ordination

All sorts of things could fit into this category, which might be useful to encourage teamworking skills amongst your learners. For example:

1) Shoot a target to release a lock (physical, or using laser pointers).

2) Use a fishing rod (with magnet or hook) to retrieve an object.
3) Get a ball bearing from one end of a maze to another in order to trigger a lock.

Combine the physical challenge with hidden information (e.g. the person with the fishing rod can't see the object), so that other members of the group have to help complete the challenge.

Hearing / Sound
Use sound to either reveal clues, or to be the puzzle in their own right.

This could be done through a soundtrack (e.g. names of tracks or artists being the clue), noise signalling something hidden (e.g. a sound that is set off when you go near an object), or a lock being triggered by the players tapping a rhythm / playing the correct notes (simple electronic locks can be created do this).

Light
A really common thing to use in escape rooms is invisible ink, combined with a UV light that reveals the hidden writing. It could also be more subtle though, such as spot lighting (or coloured lighting) that highlights clues. The pens and lights required can be cheaply bought at ways of marking your goods for security reasons (or slightly more bizarrely, showing up urine!).

Logic puzzles

A set of clues that combine logically in order to give the solution to a question. This type is often seen in books of logic puzzles solved by filling in a grid to work out the missing pieces of information (e.g. Jane is older than John. Scarlett is 25… etc, etc!).

Adapt these in an educational escape room so that subject knowledge must also be deployed to solve the logic puzzles.

Matchmaking

A type of puzzle where pairing up items from two lists, reveals the answer. Letters or numbers between the lists reveal the answer when the items are linked correctly. This could suit question / answer type lists.

For example, one list of sources of information (book, newspaper, academic journal, etc.), the second list containing some attributes (normally 50,000 words or longer, often published daily, normally peer-reviewed). If you draw a straight line between the correct pairs, they each cross one letter or number (from the set in the middle). All the letters or numbers so crossed give the solution!

Mazes

Move an item along a maze to trigger an action. It could be physically moving something through a physical maze that triggers an electronic lock (or frees an item!), or using the directions to open a directional lock (up, down, left, right). The maze could even represent steps in a process in an educational escape room, to check (or reinforce) knowledge of that process.

Maths
Often part of other puzzles, you can set simple maths puzzles that need to be solved when the numbers have been revealed in some way. This is also a convenient way of reinforcing basic maths skills as part of another lesson.

Message Puzzles
There are various types of these, where information you need is hidden within another message.

The simplest form is an acrostic puzzle, where the first letter of each word (or sentence, or line, or paragraph!) spells out a clue or solution to the puzzle. There are several variations of this, including using the last letters (rather than first), the middle letters, or even the 1st letter of the first word, 2nd of the 2nd word, etc.

Another simple one is a book cipher, where you give a series of numbers that refer to a place in a book (such as page, line, word), and working through those series of numbers will reveal a hidden message.

Pattern recognition
Seeing patterns within a whole, which reveal the clue. For example:
1) Visualising shapes from abstract components (to form letters, numbers, or arrows).

2) Showing sequences with gaps (where the gaps represent the solution to a puzzle).
3) Optical illusions, which when looked at in the correct way, reveal information.

Finding the gaps in a sequence (2) could particularly suit educational activities, where they are expected to have knowledge of a series already.

Physical agility
It is hard to see how physical puzzles fit into educational escape rooms, except as part of a teambuilding exercise. It might involve trying to move through a space without triggering a trip wire, or a light sensor.

Red Herrings
Not really puzzles in their own right, but items that look like puzzles, or clues to puzzles, but are designed to distract the player from the true solution.

These can be incredibly annoying, so use sparsely, if at all, and make sure you have an educational point you are making if you do choose to use them. Some poor quality escape rooms use red herrings to delay people completing the room, where a better room would rely on puzzles that progress the room instead.

Research
Carrying out research is an obvious one to fit into educational research rooms. You make sure that information sources are available in the room (or via the web from that room) that

must be interrogated to answer a question.

A great example of this was "Treasure Hunt" on Channel 4 in the 1980s, where contestants solved puzzles that allowed them to direct Anneka Rice to locations using the resources available to them in the room!

Riddles
A very traditional type of puzzle, riddles can give answers to reveal the next step, or the word required to open a lock.

For example (from the Hobbit):
Alive without breath,
As cold as death,
Never thirsty, ever drinking,
Dressed in mail, never clinking.
Answer: A Fish

Searching for hidden information
A very common type of puzzle found in escape rooms. It can be good to get people exploring the space in which the activity takes place, but might be annoying if heavily relied upon. Rather than physical objects that are hidden, this may be writing on walls, mirrors that change when you get close to them, information embedded in images, etc.

Searching for physical objects
This is very common in escape rooms, but can quickly get annoying if heavily relied upon. It encourages people to explore the space well (as the "hidden information" above),

but including moving and interacting with objects. It could be said that a certain amount of this (particularly early on) encourages players to feel comfortable interacting with a room. Hidden objects can be anything from keys, to parts of puzzles, to locked boxes.

Symbol substitution
This is a common, easy to create type of puzzle.

Simpler than a cipher, this is a straightforward swapping of a word, number, or symbol for another. This may be using standard languages or codes (morse code, sign language, numbers spelled out in another language), or symbols made up by yourself.

It is important to make sure a key to the symbols is available in the room!

Teamwork
Most escape rooms are impossible without good communication and teamwork between the players. From the very basic things like letting each other know what they find in the room, to passing information out of sight, or physically forming connections and working together to solve puzzles, teamwork lays underneath all escape room activities. Make sure your educational escape rooms works to build teamworking, not cause arguments that damage it!

Traditional word puzzles
An easy to create type of puzzle is a word search, or

crossword, which reveal the solution when completed. These also suit educational rooms as they can be used to check subject knowledge (or involve research to find out such knowledge), in order to complete the puzzle.

As well as standard shaped word searches and crosswords, there are lots of variations if you need to make it more complicated!

Prototyping

Now we get onto the actual making of your educational escape room! Before this stage, you should have set the learning objectives, thought about the constraints that will apply, about what sort of story or setting your activity will take place within, and what (vague) structure you will follow.

Make sure you have some prototyping materials to hand (see below!).

Now, look at your objectives one at a time. Consider some puzzles (either from the outlines above, or your own experience) that you may be able to use to meet one of your learning objectives. As soon as you have a germ of an idea… start making it. It is important not to spend too much time thinking before making, as the act of making itself will help you work it out much more effectively (this is embodied cognition, or thinking with your hands).

Once you have an idea physically worked out (or electronically if doing an online puzzle), note the outline of the puzzle and its solution.

If you feel this meets the entirety of a learning objective, then move onto the next one, if not, start to work on another puzzle to complete that learning objective.

Carry on working through the learning objectives and puzzles until you feel you have met all the objectives you set.

At this stage, try to fit them together into a "whole" organisation, and sketch out the overall puzzle organisation, referring to each puzzle as you go. You should now have a set of puzzles and an idea of how they fit together sketched out.

Do not try and get the puzzles into a completely finished state, but one where the puzzles will just about work! This is the stage where you can get the first playtesting done.
Go between playtesting and prototyping to slowly build your puzzles, the story / theme, and your other materials towards their finished state. As the puzzles start to have the rough edges knocked from them, you can spend more time on the design and the look of them, which isn't worth doing in the first playtest.

Expect to go back and forth several times while your escape room slowly moves towards being ready to use with "real" learners!

Towards the end of this process, start to think about "**Clues and hints**". That is, how can you structure and deliver hints or clues to the learners and what you may need to prepare ready to give out.

Also at the end of the prototyping stage, prepare on a single piece of paper or board a summary of your escape room activity. Make sure you cover the organisation / structure of the puzzles, a brief description and answer to each of the puzzles, and preferably a spare lock for each puzzle (if using padlocks). You could also include a key to any pre-prepared hints on the same board. This summary will make it easier for you to reset the activity after each group has finished.

Playtesting
This is a really important stage, and as mentioned above, will repeat several times. The first time you may want friends or colleagues to playtest for you, before moving onto people who are the equivalent of your final learners at the latter stages. Below are a few things to look for during these repeated playtesting sessions.

Breaking things
Escape rooms break. Lots. Look for materials that tempt playtesters into trying to force, spend a lot of time fiddling with, or which generally seem to suffer from a lot of handling. You may need to make these more robust, even if they don't actually break during testing.

(De)briefings
As well as trying out your "normal" debriefing, so an extra one after each playtest. Ask questions like:
- Did they understand what to do after the initial briefing at the start of the game?

- Did they feel satisfied that the "normal" debriefing answered any questions they had?
- Did they feel that they had learnt anything from the activity?
- What would they change if they had the choice?

Differentiation / levels
Where did people get stuck with puzzles that were simply too hard? Where there any that seemed unchallenging and too easy for your testers?

Even if you are happy you seem to have got the puzzles working well, consider how you could adjust the puzzles (or hints for the puzzles), to make the game suitable for different levels of activity.

Distractions
Look for where the players seem to have spent a lot of time. Are they learning anything there? Are they getting unnecessarily frustrated?

Consider how you could redesign the puzzles and your props, so that more of their time is spent on the valuable learning activities in the game. Think about if there are any unintended Red Herrings in the room, and how you could design them out.

Involvement of the team
Do all of your playtesters seem to be involved? Are there periods where people are stood around with nothing to do, while one or two people are busy?

Look for these and consider re-arranging the flow of the puzzles so that everyone has something to do. Playtest with differing numbers of players if necessary to check this.

Puzzle mix
Are there any puzzles which stand out as confusing to your playtesters? Were there too many of the same type of puzzle, leading to some of them getting bored? Were there any points where your playtesters consistently need a hint as they didn't know what to do next? Which were your playtesters favourites out of the puzzles, or were there any they didn't like?

Consider these to tweak the balance of the game and perhaps change a puzzle if necessary.

Clues and Hints
In commercial escape rooms, we see several different ways of delivering hints or extra clues. For our educational rooms, I'll assume we will be relatively low tech, which means we need to consider when we give clues and hints more than how! You can either give hints when players ask for them, or when you think they need them. You can come into the room and deliver them in person, or even leave them with the players in sealed envelopes (or online), with a time penalty given for each hint accessed.

Giving hints only when asked for may suit competitive players, who want to succeed on their own and "beat" the game. They may be disgruntled if they feel you have helped too much.

For most educational rooms, I'd suggest that you use your own discretion when you give hints– you want most people to finish (or nearly finish) the game, otherwise they won't have worked through all the learning objectives you've set.
Be careful though, and only give the minimum number of clues to make sure they can complete the room. Ideally they will only complete it with seconds of time to spare! Try to work out roughly how long each puzzle takes during playtesting so that you know when players are falling behind, then you can fine tune your timings of the hints accordingly. I'd also suggest that you use hints to allow for different levels of ability in your groups. Make sure that your puzzles suit the higher ability students, then use hints to make the puzzles easier for lower ability groups.

To be consistent, or to enable other people to deliver your escape room, you may want to consider preparing hints in advance.

Prepare your hints after the initial playtesting, so you have a clearer idea of where they may struggle to either understand your puzzles, or to solve them. This will allow you to plan more appropriate hints than if you had prepared them at an earlier stage.

Briefing / Debriefing

It is important in all escape room type activities to give a good briefing at the start to let people know what to expect from the room.

Three possible ways are listed here, but whichever method you use, make sure you also flag up some basic rules ("don't touch x", "Don't move that heavy cupboard", etc.), even in the "self-discovery" method. This should be done in a way that is both as obvious as possible for the players, but also as consistent as possible within the game narrative.

At the end, also make sure you have a plan for debriefing the players. Anyone who fails on a puzzle will want to know why and how they could solve it, as well as how close they were to finishing. For an educational game, this is also your opportunity to reinforce the learning activity. Make sure you plan your debrief carefully and cover all your learning objectives.

Script

This method involves a pre-written script that is read out (or provided for players to read), explaining the upcoming activity.

This method is simple, can provide consistency in briefings even when someone else acts as a gamemaster on your behalf, and gives an opportunity to ask questions afterwards.

Self-discovery
Provide no briefing (beyond a few basic groundrules), but instead let the details of the story slowly reveal themselves as the game unfolds.

This is hard to do effectively, while providing a consistent performance for all your players.

Video
Instead of a script, this method is a pre-prepared video that everyone watches before starting your activity.

This can provide a richer experience, fitting in with the theme or narrative of the game, while providing a consistent set of information to all players, even when you are not available to run the activity. It involves extra work compared to a script!

Further Information
This final section includes some further reading and links to resources that you might find useful, lists of starter materials to use in your prototyping, and some brief notes on clues and hints for your activity.

Starter materials
This isn't a list of materials I think you should use in your room, but a list to get you started prototyping!

Add to this list as you see fit, but it should allow you to mock up a range of puzzles, even if you require extra kit to make the "real" puzzles. All of these materials are widely available, including from sites such as Amazon.

Several 3 and 4 digit padlocks	These are cheap to buy! Make sure you reset them to 0000 if you end up not using them in your final puzzle.
Several "word lock" style padlocks	These generally have 4 or 5 letters that you form into a word (or random series of letters) to open. Get more than one make to give you more choice with the letter combinations and reset them if you end up not using them.
A directional padlock	These can be a bit annoying, but at least move you away from numbers / letters answers for every puzzle. They are padlocks that allow you to choose up, down, left, right (or whatever symbol you add to them) in a long series.
Several lockable boxes or bags	Cheap tool boxes often come with space to fit a padlock (& may come in a set which fit inside each other!), or cheap softwood boxes can have small hasps fitted for padlocks. Look out for cheap bags where the zip pullers include holes large enough to seal them with a padlock.
UV pen and torch	Easy way of creating hidden writing! Often sold as security pens. Make sure you get permanent ones – some are only temporary and slowly fade over time.
Sticky notes	Preferably large ones! These are great for playing with ideas in rough format.

Blank playing cards	Can get these from some game sites, but also from the likes of Amazon. Just like sticky notes, they suit moving around and playing with your ideas.
Nice pens!	I use sharpies – they can write on lots of different surfaces, so are nice for prototyping.
A "lockout" style hasp.	These go onto a box to lock it, but can take multiple padlocks, all of which need to be removed to open it. They let you have multiple pathways come together in a really simple way.
A favourite dictionary	Makes your life easier when thinking of word puzzles! Online or in print.
Sheets of acetate.	Useful for various things, but especially for colouring in / writing on (or printing on in the final version) and combining with other materials to reveal hidden clues.
Sheets of card	Useful for so many things!
Scissors / craft knife	If you haven't made a mess cutting things up, you've not had enough fun making your prototypes ;-)
Plenty of paper	An assortment – e.g. graph paper may make it easier for you to prototype some word puzzles.

References

Blair, S. & Rillo, M. (2016). *How to Facilitate Meetings & Workshops Using the LEGO Serious Play Method.* London: ProMeet.

Brown, S. L., & Vaughan, C. C. (2010). *Play: how it shapes the brain, opens the imagination, and invigorates the soul* New York: Avery.

Caillois, R., & Barash, M. (2001). *Man, play, and games.* Urbana: University of Illinois Press.

Chalmers, M. (2008). Lessons from the academy: actuating active mass-class information literacy instruction. *Reference Services Review*, 36 (1), pp.23-38.

Chang, C., Hsu, C., & Chen, I. (2013). The relationship between the playfulness climate in the classroom and student creativity. *Quality & Quantity*, 47(3), 1493-1510

Chickering, Arthur W. and Gamson Zelda F. (1987). *Seven principles for good practice in undergraduate education.* Retrieved from:
http://honolulu.hawaii.edu/intranet/committees/FacDevCom/guidebk/teachtip/7princip.htm

CILIP. (2018). *Definition of Information Literacy.*
https://infolit.org.uk/ILdefinitionCILIP2018.pdf

Cooper, M. K. (1996). *Play as a component of the adult educational experience*. Paper presented at the Proceedings of the Fifteenth Annual Midwest Research-to-Practice Conference in Adult, Continuing, and Community Education.

Csikszentmihalyi, M. (1991). *Flow: The psychology of optimal experience.* New York: HarperPerennial

De Koven, B (2014). A playful path. Halifax, Canada: ETC Press.

Deterling, S. (2017). Alibis for adult play: A Goffmanian account of escaping embarrassment in adult play. *Games and Culture*, Online first, pp. 1-20. https://doi.org/10.1177/1555412017721086

Francis, P. (2009). *Inspiring writing in art and design: taking a line for a write.* Bristol, UK: Intellect.

Gauntlett, D. (2011). *Making is connecting: the social meaning of creativity, from DIY and knitting to YouTube and Web 2.0.* Cambridge: Polity.

Gibbs, G. (1988). *Learning by doing: A guide to teaching and learning methods.* London: Further Education Unit.

Glenn, P. Knapp, M. (1987). The interactive framing of play in adult conversations. *Communication Quarterly*, 35 (1), pp. 48-66.

Goffman, E. (1967). *Interaction ritual; essays in face-to-face behavior.* United States: Doubleday.

Goffman, E. (1971). *The presentation of self in everyday life.* London: Pelican Books.

Goffman, E. (1986). *Frame analysis: An essay on the organization of experience* (Northeastern University Press ed.). Boston: Northeastern University Press.

Koh, A (2014). The political power of play. *Hybrid Pedagogy.* Retrieved from: http://www.digitalpedagogylab.com/hybridped/political-power-of-play/

Kristiansen, P., & Rasmussen, R. (2014). *Building a Better Business Using the Lego Serious Play Method.* New Jersey: John Wiley & Sons Inc.

McGonigal, J. (2012). *Reality is broken: why games make us better and how they can change the world.* London: Jonathan Cape.

Pritchard, A. (2007). *Effective teaching with internet technologies: pedagogy and practice.* London: Paul Chapman.

Pritchard, A. (2008). *Ways of Learning: learning theories and learning styles in the classroom,* 2nd Edition. Abingdon, Oxon: David Fulton.

Selinker, M. & Snyder, T. (2013). *Puzzlecraft*. New York: Sterling

Van Vleet, M. & Feeney, B. (2015). Play behavior and Playfulness in Adulthood. *Social and Personality Psychology Compass*. 9(11), pp. 630-643. http://dx.doi.org/10.1111/spc3.12205

Walsh, A. and Inala, P. (2010). *Active Learning Techniques for Librarians: Practical Examples.* Chandos: Cambridge.

Walsh, A. and Coonan, E. (2013). *Only Connect ... Discovery pathways, library explorations, and the information adventure.* Innovative Libraries, Huddersfield.

Walsh, A. (2014). The potential for using gamification in academic libraries in order to increase student engagement and achievement. *Nordic Journal of Information Literacy in Higher Education*, 6 (1). pp. 39-51. http://eprints.hud.ac.uk/21134/

Walsh, A. and Clementson, J. (2017). *Reasons to play in Higher Education.* In: The Power of Play - Voices from the Play Community. CounterPlay, Aarhus, Denmark, pp. 181-187.

Walsh, A (2017). Making Escape Rooms for Educational Purposes: A Workbook. Huddersfield: Innovative Libraries.

West, S. E., Hoff, E., Carlsson, I. (2016). Play and productivity: Enhancing the creative climate at workplace meetings with play cues. *American Journal of Play*, 9(1), pp. 71-85.

Wilson, F. (1999). *The Hand*. Vintage books edition. New York: Random House.

Wilson, M. (2002). Six views of embodied cognition. *Psychonomic bulletin & review,* 9(4), 625-636. doi: 10.3758/BF03196322

Useful organisations and conferences

Below are a few UK or European organisations and conferences that may be useful in developing and sharing your practice, based on my personal experience.

ALT-PLSIG[26]
The Association for Learning Technology Playful Learning Special Interest Group. Free membership for those in the Association for Learning Technology (ALT), which is in turn free for most people in UK Higher Education Institutions! Has a mixture of face to face meetings and virtual meetings. Primarily focussed on:
- The use of all types of games, digital and traditional, online and real world.
- The practice, as well as the theory, of play and learning.
- The use of playful appraoches with adults, in formal and informal contexts.

CILIP ILG[27]
The Chartered Institute of Library and Information Professionals Information Literacy Group. Free membership for those in CILIP. As part of focussing on Information Literacy, they include the teaching of this, and many of its members are interested in game based learning.

---

[26] https://www.alt.ac.uk/about-alt/special-interest-and-members-groups/playful-learning
[27] https://infolit.org.uk/

Counterplay[28]

This is a conference dedicated to bringing about a more playful society and can be helpful in expanding a practitioners viewpoint to encompass wider areas, particularly around the use of play as opposed to quite strictly controlled game like activities.

DMLL[29]

The Disruptive Media Learning Lab. Although primarily for Coventry University, they put a great deal of materials online. These include examples of playful learning materials and guides on how to use such an approach.

LILAC: The Information Literacy Conference[30]

This annual conference often includes game based learning approaches aimed at library professionals. It is the conference of CILIP ILG.

Playful Learning Conference[31]

This conference is "pitched at the intersection of learning and play for adults" and normally includes representation by library professionals. It is organised by the same people who run the ALT-PLSIG.

---

[28] http://www.counterplay.org/

[29] https://dmll.org.uk/

[30] http://www.lilacconference.com/

[31] http://conference.playthinklearn.net/blog/

Appendix – Benefits of playing in HE

The next few pages contain a comic written by me and illustrated by Jonny Clementson and first published as a chapter in "The Power of Play – Voices from the Play Community".

It was an attempt to write a chapter on the benefits of, and the reasons to, play in Higher Education in a playful way. The chapter is available online[32], but it's been shrunk slightly to fit on the pages below!

Walsh, A. and Clementson, J. (2017). *Reasons to play in Higher Education*. In: The Power of Play - Voices from the Play Community. CounterPlay, Aarhus, Denmark, pp. 181-187.

---

[32] http://eprints.hud.ac.uk/id/eprint/31686/

PLAY AND PLAYFULNESS IN HIGHER EDUCATION.
A COMIC ARGUMENT

ANDREW WALSH (TEXT) +
JONNY CLEMENTSON (ILLUSTRATOR)

THERE IS A LOT OF PRESSURE ON HIGHER EDUCATION
INSTITUTIONS AND IT CAN BE HARD TO FIND SPACE FOR PLAY
AND PLAYFULNESS. BUT WHAT IF THE BENEFITS OF PLAY AND
THE INTERESTS OF STUDENTS, UNIVERSITIES, AND THE
GOVERNMENT COINCIDED? THIS SHORT COMIC ARGUES THAT
THEY DO, AND THAT PLAT CAN HELP HIGHER EDUCATION
INSTITUTIONS EFFECTIVELY MEET THE NEEDS OF ALL PARTIES.

FROM THE PERSPECTIVE OF **UK HIGHER EDUCATION**, IT CAN FEEL **DIFFICULT** TO FIND SPACE AND JUSTIFICATION FOR **PLAY**. "UNIVERSITIES MUST DO MORE TO DEMONSTRATE THEY ADD **REAL AND LASTING VALUE** FOR ALL STUDENTS", LARGELY DEFINED AS PRODUCING STUDENTS "**READY TO CONTRIBUTE TO SOCIETY**" AND TO BUSINESSES KEEN TO EMPLOY INCREASING NUMBERS OF **SKILLED GRADUATES.** *

*JOHNSON, 2015, MINISTER FOR UNIVERSITIES AND SCIENCE

PRESSURES ON HIGHER EDUCATION

"VALUE" IS LINKED TO HOW MUCH **MONEY** STUDENTS WILL EARN UPON GRADUATION. THE **TEACHING EXCELLENCE FRAMEWORK** WILL CONTROL **UNIVERSITIES' INCOME** BASED ON:

SATISFACTION SURVEYS

RETENTION

"GRADUATE" EMPLOYMENT

ACADEMIC ACHIEVEMENT

RECRUITMENT PRESSURE MEANS LEAGUE TABLES HAVE **INFLATED** IMPORTANCE.

EMPLOYERS WANT GRADUATES WHO CAN **COMMUNICATE** WELL...

...WORK AS A **TEAM**...

...HAVE **TECHNICAL SKILLS**...

...AND HAVE **LEADERSHIP** AND **MANAGEMENT** SKILLS.

143

WHAT ARE PLAY, PLAYFULNESS AND GAMES?

PLAY AND GAMES SIT ON A **SPECTRUM** FROM "**FREE**" IMAGINATIVE PLAY TO HIGHLY **STRUCTURED** GAMES.

EDUCATIONAL GAMES CAN INTRODUCE PLAY INTO **H.E.** WITH GREATER OR LESSER AMOUNTS OF "**PLAY**" IN THEM.

EVEN QUITE **FORMAL GAME** CAN BE PLAYFUL IF YOU LE PEOPLE **ADAPT** THE RULE AS THEY GO ALONG

HUIZINGA DEFINES PLAY AS: WE MIGHT CALL IT A **FREE ACTIVITY** STANDING QUITE CONSCIOUSLY OUTSIDE '**ORDINARY**' LIFE AS BEING ' NOT SERIOUS' BUT AT THE SAME TIME **ABSORBING** THE PLAYER INTENSELY AND UTTERLY. IT IS AN ACTIVITY CONNECTED WITH **NO MATERIAL INTEREST**, AND **NO PROFIT** CAN BE GAINED BY IT. IT PROCEEDS WITHIN ITS OWN PROPER BOUNDARIES OF TIME AND SPACE ACCORDING TO **FIXED RULES** AND IN AN ORDERLY MANNER. IT PROMOTES THE FORMATION OF **SOCIAL GROUPINGS**...

PLAYFULNESS IS AN ATTRIBUTE IN SPACE OR AN ATTITUDE THAT **ENCOURAGES PLAY**.

PLAY IS OFTEN THOUGHT OF AS HAPPENING IN A "**MAGIC CIRCLE**". THE SENSE OF **SELF** IS **SUPPRESSED**, PLAYERS CAN THINK FROM **DIFFERENT** POINTS OF VIEW, PEOPLE WANT TO **START** AND **CONTINUE** PLAYING, **SOCIAL GROUPING** IS PROMOTED."

SOMEONE WITH A **PLAYFUL ATTITUDE** TENDS TO THINK "CAN I PLAY WITH THIS?", "HOW CAN I HAVE FUN?", "WHAT **ALTERNATIVE** USES CAN I PUT XYZ TO?".

144

WHAT PLAY IS GOOD FOR

PLAYFUL **SPACES** HELP THE **EXPLORATION** OF IDEAS.
YOU CAN DO **ANYTHING**, BE **ANYONE**.
THIS IS WHERE **NEW KNOWLEDGE** COMES FROM

GAMES HAVE A LONG PEDIGREE IN **EDUCATION** FOR **PRACTICING SKILLS**. THEY NOT ONLY LET US PRACTICE THE **RIGHT** THINGS TO DO, BUT LEARN THE CONSEQUENCES OF THE **WRONG** THINGS AS WELL".

SO **COUNTERPLAY** (PLAYING "**AGAINST**" A GAME'S **INTENTION**) CAN EVEN MAKE GAMES MORE PLAYFUL AND **DEEPENS LEARNING**.

GAMES AND PLAY ARE GREAT FOR **ACTIVE LEARNING**, WITH GAMES SCAFFOLDING THE **LEARNING PROCESS**.

CREATIVE AND **PLAYFUL** ACTIVITIES ENABLE **LEARNING** AND **REFLECTION**.

SUMMING UP

THE **GOVERNMENT** AND **EMPLOYERS** WANT GRADUATES TO **STAY** AT UNIVERSITY, GET GOOD **QUALIFICATIONS**, BE "**SATISFIED**", BE GOOD **TEAM PLAYERS**, TO **COMMUNICATE** WELL, HAVE WHICH SHOULD LEAD TO **BETTER JOBS** AND **ENGAGED CITIZENS**.

PLAY HELPS PEOPLE FEEL **INVOLVED** AS PART OF A GROUP (WHICH HELPS **RETENTION**), SEE THINGS FROM **ALTERNATIVE** POINTS OF VIEW, PRACTICE **SKILLS**, ENJOY LEARNING (WHICH HELPS QUALIFICATIONS AND CREATION OF **KNOWLEDGE**), BE "**CHALLENGED**" IN THEIR LEARNING (AN IMPORTANT PART OF STUDENT SATISFACTION), LEARN GOOD **COMMUNICATION** AND **TEAM WORKING** SKILLS (VITAL FOR GRADUATE EMPLOYMENT). BUT ALSO SKILLS THAT ARE **VITAL** FOR A **CREATIVE**, **EMPATHETIC**, **REFLECTIVE**, AND **TOLERANT** CITIZENSHIP.

LAST, BUT NOT LEAST, PLAY IS OFTEN **FUN**. THE GOVERNMENT, EMPLOYERS, UNIVERSITIES, AND THE LIKE MIGHT NOT **CARE** ABOUT FUN, BUT IF WE CAN HAVE FUN AT THE SAME TIME AS MEETING ALL THE OTHER NEEDS, THEN **WHY NOT?**

More from Innovative Libraries Press.

"Only connect ... discovery pathways, library explorations, and the information adventure" represents the richness of information discovery. We present a range of information discovery journeys, from reflections upon formal search processes to a library fairy story.

Standard "list price" £19.95.

ISBN: 978-0957665217

The Mini Book of Teaching Tips for
Librarians. 2nd Edition.
Andrew Walsh

The 2nd edition of "The Mini Book of Teaching Tips for
Librarians" (A6, 100 pages long) is a series of ~70 teaching tips
and ideas for librarians. Most tips are just 1 page long, making
it easy to dip into in order to get tips and ideas to improve
your teaching.

Standard list price £9.95.

ISBN: 9781911500117

"Writing Essays By Pictures" uses visual analogies to explain all the bits that go into researching and writing at degree level - particularly those steps that often remain hidden to students at their first try.

Writing Essays by Pictures explains the basics of academic research to the beginner - and to people who have always wished for a way to make these things visual... and fun!

Standard "list price" £15

Print ISBN: 978-0957665224